Notes from the 59th Floor

Notes from the 59th Floor

A Year's Worth of Thoughts and Reflections on China

by Sam Levy

MORGAN FIELD BOOKS

First published in paperback in 2025

Paperback ISBN 978-1-0369-3284-8

To my dad

Contents

Introduction

I never set out to write a book about China. If nothing else, I figured I'd come back with a year's worth of wild stories for the pub and some bragging rights about having "done something different." But even now, long after my visa's expiration date, I still catch myself jotting on bus tickets, thumbing through faded journal entries, and replaying grainy phone clips of moments so bizarre I still wonder if they actually happened.

People ask the question all the time: *What was China really like?* They want to know the *truth*. This book is my best shot at answering that question. But here's the catch: I only ever saw one version of China—*my* version. The one experienced by a stubborn, broke barely-adult from the UK, armed with nothing but a battered suitcase and a string of brash decisions. I never saw 'the real China.' Honestly, I don't think anyone has. But I saw *a* China—dazzling, maddening, terrifying, hilarious, and unforgettable.

The second question I get is: *Why?* Why on Earth would I elect to do such a thing? *You do realise they eat dogs, right?* And then I tell them I went because I just felt like it. *You do realise their government probably has loads of information on you now?* Yes, I do.

And, dear Communist Party of China, if you're reading, please note that I am completely unimportant! Nothing about the ruminations in this book is meant to be inflammatory or even inspiring—at least, not in a political sense. Hopefully, readers find this book interesting, eye-opening, and thought-provoking. While it is critical of aspects of life in China, it is also celebratory and, in some ways, commendatory. I could just as easily have written a positive-negative reflection on any other nation in the world, not least of which my own.

In any case, to answer the question, I decided to go because I was as young, zealous, and optimistic as I was fed up, cynical, and pessimistic. It was the quarrelsome marriage of these two sides of my brain that somehow led me to the People's Republic of China.

If you're looking for a definitive travel guide or a list of 'top ten must-sees,' then look elsewhere. Instead, these are stories and snapshots: Awkward first conversations, back-alley meals that changed my definition of 'spicy,' neon-lit nights that left me questioning everything I knew, and yes, my critical evaluation, a review of the nation from my limited perspective, a review that is both expository and fault-finding; positive and negative. In a word? *Honest*. I will tell you about China's undivulged successes, while also airing its dirty laundry.

Each chapter captures a single episode—a vivid, real-life moment that reveals something bigger, perhaps leaving you with more questions than answers. Alone, they're just observations. Together, they become something like an insider's map of contradiction: China as riddle, as paradox, as a place that is always both more and less than you expect.

So, let's start at the beginning: On the plane journey, with an old man in seat 25-B, and the surreal, stratospheric conversation that became my first real schooling on China. Along the way, we'll uncover hard truths, navigate chopstick mishaps, and try (and fail) to define what it means to understand another country.

Only in studying the East can we truly understand the West. Whether you romanticise China, demonise it, love it, or fear it, I'm sure we can all agree that China is *significant*. It is one of the most important countries in the world. Whether you've already been and are interested in another traveller's take, whether you are looking for reasons to venture there, or whether you are looking for reasons to stay safely at home, I'm sure you will find them in this book.

These are my notes from the 59th floor. Welcome to China, told through the shaky yet vivid lens of a young, British expat.

The Old Man in Seat 25-B

I'm not even going to bother ordering these chapters chronologically. (I guess the order will be determined instead by subconscious associations and the varying strength of my coffee.) That being said, for this first chapter, it makes sense to start at the beginning with the old man in seat 25-B, the person with whom I had my very first conversation in Chinese.

Before boarding the plane, I had five phrases to my name: *Hello. Goodbye. How are you? Good. Not good.*

By the time we landed in Chongqing, I had a whole arsenal. Words and phrases like **tài rè le** (*too hot*), after the man warned me about Chongqing's climate. Now that I think about it, the old man didn't exactly fill me with confidence about the city I had been arbitrarily assigned to. He also warned me about **tài duō rén** (*too many people*). Indeed, Chongqing turned out to be home to thirty million people, making it three times more populous than the largest city in the UK, from which we'd just taken off.

And if that wasn't enough, the old man—whose name I never actually learned—also described Chongqing as "noisy and scary." He didn't speak a lick of English during the entire eleven-hour flight, but using a steady stream of gestures, hand signals, and pointing, he taught me close to a hundred words.

To demonstrate **fēijī** (*aeroplane*), he spread his arms like wings and pointed out the window.

To teach me **chéngshì** (*city*), he tapped each dot on the digital flight map in front of us, repeating the word until I raised my eyebrows and gave a half-comprehending nod of recognition.

We interacted for just under six hours, which is, coincidentally, the same duration as a British school day. And it was, without question, one of the most useful 'school days' I've ever had. I learned a great deal, not only about China and its geography, but also about language acquisition. In fact, I can summarise it into four main lessons:

1) *If you want to learn a language properly, don't fall back on English in the process. English is your enemy.*
2) *If you want to learn a language quickly, speak as often as possible with anyone willing to share a conversation with you. Don't be shy. Don't be a perfectionist. Mistakes are to language what a journey is to a destination. Errors are part of the fun, and errors are beautiful.*
3) *Situations you can't leave (i.e., aboard a moving aeroplane) are your friend.*
4) *Put down the phone, delete the apps, and learn from real life. The world is your greatest teacher, and it's waiting for you.*

Those who know me might consider me a bit of a language nerd, a wannabe linguist if not a true polyglot. While I had previously managed to learn French, half-learn Russian, and just about get through A-Level Spanish, I had no ambitions when it came to Mandarin. Before my time in China, I was fascinated with languages, but during my stay, that's when I truly fell in love with them. This love came to me in a stream of feelings: The feeling of connecting with a stranger—a stranger who would have otherwise drifted meekly beyond my eye-line into the void of what-could've-been. Then there's the feeling of correctly stringing together your first semi-complex sentence, with correct intonation, accompanied by appropriate gestures, pauses, breathwork, and cadence. There's the feeling of learning something you would never have otherwise learned, helping someone you would never have been able to help, seeing the world in a way you would never have seen.

When you learn a foreign language, not only does the language become a part of you, *you* become a part of *it*. It's true. As a matter of fact, you enter the intangible yet ever so real and world-changing conglomerate of the language itself. Chinese, or whichever language you dare to study, is an accumulation of hundreds, if not thousands, of years of history. Chinese is every person who has ever spoken, heard, thought, or dreamt a word of the language. Chinese is every singular and molecular effect that its style of communication has on the world, as is English, as is Navajo, as is Makaton, as is every other form of communication imaginable. Wolves howl, crickets chirp, and cotton-top tamarins whisper. It is *all* a very real part of this magnificent, multilingual world. And though you may never be able to share a dialogue with a wolf, or even a domestic dog, it is easier than you think to learn another language (a human one), and you don't need to learn much to be a part of it. You don't need to be a genius either, despite popular belief. You don't need to be a savant. All you need to do is enjoy it, all of it, including the mistakes and drawbacks.

For me, this discovery began in seat 25-A, next to the old man, to whom I am eternally grateful. You see, when the plane landed, it was not the end of my journey... It was the beginning.

The old man was my first taste of Chinese hospitality, patience, and willingness not only to teach youngsters but to learn from them. If you'll allow me to generalise, Chinese people are humble, hard-working, community-minded, and pragmatic—and without a doubt, it is the seniors who embody these characteristics most of all.

In China, in a small but not insufficient way, you are everyone's brother or sister (which I will discuss more in a later chapter), and to every old person, you are a grandson or granddaughter. This much is true so long as you allow them to be your grandparent, so long as you dare to mirror a mutual, generational respect that we have largely lost in the West.

The old man in 25-B was merely connecting in Chongqing, which is where he left me to continue his journey to see his daughter in Kunming. He was unapologetically honest about the arduous journey I was about to undertake. He made me nervous. He made me second-guess and then quadruple-guess my decision to leave the UK. Nevertheless, he was my first interaction with China. He was the first of many teachers. He was kind, caring, and patiently tenacious in his attempts to share his beautiful language with me. The way I like to see it, the old man in 25-B was my doorman, my porter, or better yet, my *concierge* at the gateways of China, and for that, I thank him.

"Things are off to a good start.
I've met and lost my first new friend already."

– Day 1

The 8D City

Chongqing is pronounced *chong-ching*, which is, as some people seem to enjoy pointing out, a very 'stereotypical-sounding' name. Yes, English has a way of bullying and butchering the name, but you'll have to take my word for it—it sounds a lot nicer in native Chinese. Now, enough about languages, let's talk about the city itself.

Actually, the city of Chongqing is not a city so much as it is an experience. A challenge. A dare. It's one of those places that insists on being described with numbers, but where numbers don't really help. Thirty million people, they say. *But what does that even mean?* Thirty-one thousand square miles. *Excuse me?* Eight urban districts. Ninety-degree cliff faces. Ninety-storey towers growing like bamboo from the mist. Two mighty rivers meeting in the centre like tangled shoelaces. I could go on.

The most helpful number I can use to paint a picture of Chongqing is the number eight. As in, eight dimensions. This term isn't scientific or even mathematical—it's meme science, internet folklore, a collective shrug by locals and expats alike to explain why nothing in this city works the way you expect it to. It attempts to recreate the feeling of the city's hundreds of layers and the mountains in which they are built. Chongqing is a labyrinth of staircases, subways, skyways, escalators, and lifts.

I lived there for a year. And yes, I got lost. Often. But it was an exciting kind of lost, it was the kind of lost you want to find—if that makes any sense at all.

Chongqing has evolved across rolling hills, sharp ridges, gorges, and valleys, which is another way of saying it has been built wherever there shouldn't, by the basic laws of physics, be a city. The result is a layout so disorienting that Google Maps has no idea what to do with it, which is why I gave up on digital maps early on. More than once, I was told I was on the second floor of a building, while also being thirty meters above ground level. There are shopping malls with twelve entrances on six different levels. Apartment blocks with elevators that go up *and* sideways (like in Harry Potter, yes). On one occasion, I found a street that was quite literally on top of another street—not a bridge, but a fully functioning road with restaurants, signage, and traffic lights, sitting comfortably on the roof of another street.

When I first arrived, I thought I could outsmart the layout with logic. Rookie mistake. Chongqing is not interested in your logic. It is governed by forces more powerful than mere urban planning: altitude, humidity, mass crowds, and the path of least resistance. You do not 'navigate' Chongqing so much as you participate in it. You give up control, let the escalators, and the crowds, and the overlapping roads take you where they will. And sometimes—most of the time—you arrive where you never intended, and it's better than anything you had planned.

That's the beauty of it.

But let's not pretend it's *all* beautiful. For one thing, it's loud. Every square metre of Chongqing comes with its own soundtrack: horns, hawkers, traffic, street karaoke, yelling merchants, construction that seems to take place exclusively at 4 a.m. On one occasion, a woman stood directly outside my flat and shouted into her phone for twenty-five minutes at full volume, and no one batted an eye. Not even the cat. Cacophony is just a part of life.

And then there's the 'air situation,' which is, I think, the nicest name I can come up with. Chongqing's climate is intensely humid for most of the year, especially in summer, when it can feel like someone wrapped the city in a damp towel and left it in the sun. You can break a sweat just by blinking. In fact, to 'break a sweat' is simply to open the window. The real question is, how do you *break out* of sweating? If you hang your washing on the balcony, it doesn't dry so much as it *acclimatises*. And when the air pollution decides to join the party—which it does, especially in winter—the city becomes a hazy bowl of soup. A dramatic, neon-lit, concrete soup.

I'd be lying if I said I didn't find it overwhelming at times. I missed fresh air. I missed silence. I missed pavements that didn't just... end. I missed the simplicity of knowing where the bus stop was and not having to take three escalators and a maze of pedestrian tunnels to reach it.

But that's the contradiction of Chongqing. The very things that wear you out are the things that give you energy, and that give the city its electricity. For all its chaos, Chongqing has a certain magnetism—not the glossy, curated charm of a tourist town, but a raw, kinetic energy that keeps you moving. It's a city that doesn't pretend to be tidy or perfect. It is not romanticised like Paris. It is not glorified like New York. And in that way, it never disappoints.

Chongqing just *is*.

Vast, alive, unapologetic. People hustle here. The elderly climb hills with shopping bags and a baby on their back with no complaint. Young couples work until midnight and come home with enough energy for a long, sociable meal with family. Children go to school for nine hours, not including extra-curricular sports and music lessons. Everything feels like it's in motion, and yet people still find time to talk to you. In that way, Chongqing feels incredibly human. No, that's wrong. It doesn't feel human. It feels *superhuman*, and that is simultaneously its greatest strength and most notable weakness.

In any case, that brings me to perhaps the most underappreciated feature of the 8D City—its people. They don't just put up with the absurdity; they *thrive* in it. They're opportunists, which is the only way to survive in an ever-expanding city. But despite their drive, they do not let it get in the way of making time (an inexplicable abundance of time) for get-togethers with family, friends, and even strangers—even foreign strangers. There is a warmth to the city that runs deeper than the hot pot, and trust me, the hot pot runs deep. (More on that later.)

Of course, there are things I never quite got used to. The vertical sprawl can be exhausting, even for the young-legged. My dad raised me to climb mountains from the moment I could walk. I wish I could say that came in handy. There were days I would get home dripping in sweat, legs aching, socks wet from a puddle I never saw coming, only to be begged by a gang of children to play basketball with them. But then I'd walk out onto the balcony at night, and the city would be glowing—not twinkling like some dainty postcard, but *glowing*, as if every building had a heartbeat. I'd hear the faint rumble of the sky-rail snaking through the hills. I'd see the bridges lit up like science fiction. And I'd think, *this is a place that doesn't care if you approve of it.* I respected that.

As much as I love dogs, I've always had a slight affinity with cats, and I think it's because of the same issue. Dogs want you to love them, they need your attention, and they want to make you happy by learning your stupid tricks—lay down, spin, paw—and that's nice, but cats don't care what you think. Chongqing is the cat of cities.

So here's my final take: Chongqing is disorienting. It's overwhelming. It's absurd, intense, humid, and sometimes unkind. It will make you shed a dozen pounds. It will give you acne. It will shake you about like a ball-in-a-maze puzzle until you are utterly lost. But it's also exhilarating. It humbles you. It teaches you to slow down, to ask for help, to accept that you don't always need to know where you're going. In Chongqing, I learned to stop being so controlling of my *own* life, let alone other people's. It's like that old saying, "Man plans, and God laughs." Because as much as mayors, architects, and developers would like to believe they plan the city, and build it, and excavate it, at some point, the city takes on a mind of its own. The city truly is alive. The city truly is an *animal.* The city truly is a character on the stage of life.

"I can't seem to find the centre of this city.
It keeps moving."

– Day 6

Never-Ending Rice

In China, especially southern China, rice is less *food* and more *metaphysical certainty*. It is both beginning and end. Alpha and omega. The default state of a breakfast, lunch, and dinner table. It's always there, even if you're not sure who asked for it. And just when you think, "Ah, good, I've made a dent in this small hill of steamed starch," someone (usually a concerned mother-figure) materialises out of nowhere and, without asking, tactically *reloads* your bowl. You are Sisyphus, and your punishment is not a boulder up a hill, but a spoon in a bowl that refuses to empty.

I could tell you the surname of the family I lived with. Seeing as the surname is shared by seventy million people (a population bigger than the UK), I would be safe using their real name without any further need for anonymity. But just to be safe, I'll choose an even more common name. Let's call them the 'Lee family.'

The Lee family was no exception to this rice rule. The rice cooker in their kitchen was roughly the size of a small car engine and was permanently on standby, like a nuclear reactor waiting to go critical. If it ever shut off, I never saw it. I have vague memories of the grandma waking up at 5:45 a.m. and mumbling something like, "Better start the rice," as if she were loading coal into a steam engine. It was a sacred ritual. A security blanket. A lifestyle. A source of national pride.

Let's begin with the basics. In Chinese, the word for food is **fàn**, which just so happens to also be the word for rice... That's really all you need to know, to be honest.

At first, I was fully on board. I'm a tolerant guy. I like carbohydrates. I'd had takeaway egg-fried rice before. I thought I knew what I was doing. But takeaway egg-fried rice is to southern Chinese rice culture what instant coffee is to a third-wave, beard-stroking, pour-over barista.

And it's not just the rice. It's the things that go *with* the rice. Some of them are, in all fairness, divine. Spicy Sichuan chicken that numbs your gums and sets off fireworks in your sinuses. Glazed aubergine with so much umami it should be illegal. Soft, off-the-bone river fish with green pepper that dances on your tongue like martial arts. Vegetables the likes of which you have never seen, lotus root, yu choy, bamboo shoots. These are the good times.

But then there's *the other stuff.*

In several restaurants frequented by my Chinese family, pig brain was not just on the menu; it was the house special. Not *a* pig brain. *Your choice* of brain, in fact, with optional toppings. You could get it steamed, stir-fried, or nestled in a hot pot like it was a dollop of tofu someone forgot to label correctly. The pig brain is, I'm not ashamed to admit, a delicacy I did *not* indulge in.

And yes, let's get it out the way: They eat dog meat. It's not as common as some Westerners would have you believe, but still a very real part of *some* people's diet—though, fortunately, not my host family's. Still, to make extra sure I didn't end up in a dog meat restaurant, one of the first words I learned was **gǒu** (*dog*).

Whether it is inherently wrong to eat dog is debatable. I remember convincing myself, at one point in time, that it is either moral to eat *any* animal or immoral to eat *any* animal. Regardless of how much flesh we consume, hopefully my readers can agree that the *way* we treat animals is often abusive, disgusting, and in the modern world, frankly, dystopian. China is no exception to this. In fact, it is among the biggest of perpetrators—but maybe that's a topic for a later chapter.

Regardless, as a Westerner who grew up in a house with dogs, in a county where practically everyone owns at least one canine (Lincolnshire), I am forever in a state of mortification when it comes to the *idea* of eating a dog. If we are to nominate only one creature, one friend, such that they cannot be eaten, then for God's sake, let it be the dog! But I will admit, only to a certain degree, that this is merely a cultural concept.

And then there was the turtle.

It started, as so many stories do, with an innocent trip to the bathroom. I'd gone downstairs to use the *other* toilet in peace, and there it was: a live turtle, swimming around in a plastic bucket. I greeted it, perhaps too optimistically. I tried not to name it, out of fear of what was to come. But we like to name things, don't we? And so, a subconscious part of me gave this particular reptile the name 'Greg.' Well, sure enough, the next day, Greg swam in quite a different way—in a bowl of soup, and very much dead. I stared into the bowl. The bowl stared back. The idea was, I suppose, to pour the Greg soup onto the rice. The endless bowl of rice.

There are many pivotal moments in China. Some of them feel like a hallucination. Most of them happen around the dinner table. Rice, it seems, is the ever-present observer of such moments. To paraphrase Shakespeare, "My rice is as boundless as the sea."

Anyway, the point is that the endless rice is a bed for many strange feasts. Breakfast was another matter entirely. In Britain, breakfast is cereal, or toast, or more often than not, nothing at all. In China? You guessed it. More rice. Soup. Fried meat. Cold noodles. Fermented eggs that look like something you'd find in a science museum. Things that can surely only be a *dinner* meal—but are being consumed with a cheery **"zǎo shàng hǎo!"** before 7 a.m.

And then there's *congee*, a rice porridge so deeply unenthusiastic about being eaten that it practically weeps as you spoon it up. I'm not sure if a food can 'slouch,' but if any can, it's congee. It took a lot to keep it down. But you get used to it, and before long, you start craving it.

But still, I knew things were getting out of hand when rice became a threat to... well, my life. After about a month of eating steamed white rice for every single meal, something in my Caucasian digestive system quietly waved the white flag. I developed what can only be described as an internal uprising. After a three-day fever and an internal rebellion that forced me into the local hospital—an experience which, for the record, involved a gastroscopy and a fierce nurse shouting the word **dùzi** (*belly*) at me repeatedly—I learned the hard way that rice contains trace levels of arsenic. It turns out eating three metric tonnes of it in four weeks is not ideal for the average Brit.

Here's the thing. Even after all that—after the turtle, the near-miss with pig brains, and the full-blown rice-induced hospitalisation—I kind of admire it. The commitment. The consistency. Not only the ability to make use of *everything* and waste absolutely *nothing*, but the sheer unwavering presence of rice in every possible situation. It's strangely comforting.

Still, I should point out that bottomless rice bowls ring with an echo of an uncomfortable past. It is important to understand that the Chinese obsession with endless rice comes from a painful history. For centuries, particularly in the previous one, millions upon millions of people died from starvation. Many of the elderly citizens of modern-day China remember counting individual grains as a child, and so twenty-first-century China's abundance of rice isn't just a preference; it's a statement. It's saying, "We're never going to go hungry again. Our grandchildren will not know what it *means* to starve. Their stomachs won't even know what it means to *rumble*."

These days, rice is reliable. Rice doesn't argue. Rice is always there for you, like a clingy but dependable ex. It's just that after a while, if you're an ungrateful Westerner like me, you start craving a bit of distance. Maybe a sandwich. Just a slice of real cheese. Chocolate that doesn't make you gag. As a coastal Brit, the thing I missed most of all was good old fish n' chips. As a matter of fact, whenever I complained of being 'homesick,' I was really just thinking about my local chippy.

To this day, I can't look at steamed rice without hearing the mechanical clunk of the cooker lid locking shut and thinking: *Oh no. It's happening again.* And yet, after I left China, and even at this very moment, I do miss something about it. Not the hospitalisation, obviously, but the ritual. The way someone would refill your bowl without asking, like a strange act of quiet affection. The steam fogging up the kitchen windows. The clink of chopsticks against porcelain. The sense that no matter what else was going on in the world around you—rain, arguments, loneliness, homesickness—there would always be rice.

"I'm starting to realise
full doesn't mean finished in this place."

– Day 12

The 5 Yellow Stars

Rice is not the only constant. There's also the flag. It's hard to overstate just how prominent the Chinese flag is in China. It's just *there.* It is, as it happens, one of surprisingly many things China and America have in common with each other. Something they wouldn't care to admit.

I'd walk past the red flag with its golden stars outside the school gates, I'd see it hung up in shop windows, and it waved at me from the sides of lorries and government buildings alike. It appeared on lapel pins, in textbooks, on souvenir mugs, and was the backdrop of many profile pictures. It crowned giant LED billboards in places like Jiefangbei and draped quietly in the corners of humble noodle shops in the countryside.

In Britain, the national flag appears when there's a sporting event, or perhaps a coronation, and then it disappears again. Many people in Britain have never flown a Union Jack in their lives, and probably never will. In China, like in parts of America, the flag is non-optional. It's not seasonal, but perennial. It blooms in every corner of public life.

At first, it caught me off guard. Not because I had a problem with it, but because of the sheer scale of its presence. There was a sense that it wasn't just a symbol—it was a participant. A kind of silent fifth, or rather, a five-starred symbol, a character in every workplace photo. Even if no one was talking about the flag, it was there. Watching.

But then again, it is a good flag, as flags go. I mean that aesthetically. The red is punchy. The gold pops. It's simple, recognisable, and even a bit regal. There's a reason it makes such an effective sticker, badge, and stage backdrop.

I once wore it on my lapel, in pin badge form, during a cultural event hosted in Chongqing, where I was asked to do a short interview about my experiences in China. It was all very staged and ceremonial, with children performing songs and dances, local dignitaries smiling from their elevated seating positions, and camera crews swivelling to catch every angle of orchestrated harmony. When it was my turn to speak, I smiled. I said positive things. Not because I was being forced to exactly, but because I knew I had to—and there's an important distinction there. I spoke about nice things because the pin badge was watching me. In many ways, I felt the flag itself was watching me, with five star-shaped eyes.

Incidentally, children salute differently to adults. I learned this during the 70th anniversary celebrations of the People's Republic of China, which I had the surreal honour of witnessing from inside the country. As I stood there in a precise column with the kids whom I had been teaching English, staring up at a twenty-foot Chinese flag flapping above the building, I watched as they all raised their right hands in unison and delivered a very specific kind of child's salute—flat palm, tilted at an angle, raised well above their heads. It was sincere, rehearsed, and strangely touching. It also made me feel out of place.

This was not my flag. It was theirs. And there I was, clapping along to patriotic songs about revolution and progress, mouthing along to lyrics I only half-understood, all under the glare of this enormous, omnipresent red rectangle. In that moment, the flag felt heavy. Not materially, but symbolically. A distillation of a very different national story.

The flag's design dates back to 1949, when the People's Republic of China was founded. The large gold star represents the Communist Party, and the four smaller stars represent the four social classes united under the party: the working class, the peasantry, the urban petite bourgeoisie, and the national bourgeoisie. They curve deferentially around the big star, angled slightly inward, like satellites orbiting a planet. It is a symbol of unity, yes, but also of hierarchy. Of loyalty. Of centralisation. Of influence and authority.

And what better way to centre the flag than to put it everywhere? In China, the flag is not something to be occasionally witnessed—it is something to be constantly respected. I'd see old men adjusting faded flags on their balconies. I'd see toddlers walking around with little ones glued to their backpacks. I even saw it carved into the foam of a coffee at a trendy fusion café. When the anniversary rolled around, you could barely move for red banners, red bunting, red paper cuttings pasted on glass doors, and endless flags planted into flower beds. It was as though the whole country had decided to throw itself a birthday party and insisted on dressing in theme.

And maybe that's not so strange. In the UK, people often avoid overt patriotism for fear of being mistaken for a hooligan or a racist. Even writing about that in this book will make some of my British readers feel uncomfortable. But in China, patriotism is state-encouraged, curriculum-integrated, and often indistinguishable from national identity. I don't mean that in a sinister way. Not entirely. For many people, the flag is simply a symbol of pride. Of how far the country has come. Of skyscrapers that rise like bamboo. Of bridges over misty rivers. Of the ability to build high-speed railways at a velocity that feels almost mythological. Patriotism, in its warmest form, is gratitude. Gratitude that things function. That development is visible. That the country survived its own history and still stands, five stars intact.

Still, it is hard not to notice the uniformity of it all. I once asked some students what their favourite colour was, and after a brief silence, one of them said, "Red." Another nodded. A third agreed. And that was that. There was no turquoise, no purple, and certainly no blue. Just red. A tidal wave of consensus. At first, I thought they were joking. But the more I asked around, the more I got the same answer. Red. And in fact, if you ask almost anyone in China what their favourite colour is, they'll say the same.

Now let's not get carried away here. It is important to remember that there are historical and cultural reasons for this. Red is associated with luck, celebration, and prosperity. It's the colour of weddings, of envelopes filled with money, of firecrackers, and plum blossoms. But when everyone gives the same answer, you can't help but wonder whether they were answering the question or just performing the answer they thought they were supposed to give. I felt that way about a lot of responses. Responses to questions about the government, about what was going on in Taiwan, about what was going on in Xinjiang. The responses sounded imitative and rehearsed, but in any case, I learned not to ask such questions. Not only did it feel dangerous to do so, but I simply couldn't bear the performance, whether it was a performance they themselves bought or not.

People were curious about me, delighted to practise their English, and often far too generous with gifts and compliments. But occasionally, I sensed something else. A pressure to play my role. To be the friendly foreigner. The cheerful guest. The silent approver of things. Wearing the flag lapel pin at the cultural event was part of that. No one forced it on me. But when someone handed it to me, I pinned it on automatically, like I was suiting up for a part in a play.

And there is a script. You are supposed to marvel at the infrastructure. You are supposed to praise the hospitality. You are supposed to contrast the safety of Chinese cities with the danger of the West. You are supposed to say that everything is "very convenient," and honestly, much of it is. I liked many things about life in China. I still do. But there is a difference between liking something and being obliged to like it.

There were moments when the flag made me feel proud, or at least, vicariously proud, distantly, in the same way you might be proud of your second cousin's GCSE results. I admired how hard they worked, how well they hosted, how devoted many were to their families and communities. I guess there is something inspiring about a country that believes in itself.

But the flag is not just a celebration. It is also a reminder. A kind of permanent presence, like the background hum of an air conditioner. You don't always notice it, but it's always there. Spectating. Framing the photo.

The future of the flag? Well, that depends on the future of China, and no one really knows where that's going, despite what the government might say. There is a sense of unstoppable rise, yes, but also a kind of controlled tightrope walk. Will the flag continue to represent prosperity and progress? Or will it come to symbolise something more brittle, more inward-looking? It depends on who you ask. It depends on how much they trust you.

I remember one moment, quite vividly. A little girl I taught asked me if we had a flag in Britain. I said yes. She asked what colour it was. I drew it for her. She squinted. "Too many colours," she said.

Maybe she was right. An unencumbered red does make a statement. It's bold. It doesn't leave room for doubt. It claims the wall, the moon, Mars, the moment, the attention. It says, "Here I am."

At the end of my time in China, I packed up my belongings and noticed the flag pin had made its way to the bottom of my drawer. I kept it. Not as propaganda, or compliance, and not as a show of support for the government... just as a souvenir, a memory, and nothing more. And maybe that's what it comes down to. The flag can also be a symbol of variance. It means different things to different people, and sometimes, different things to the same person at different times.

"The Chinese flag is red to represent bloodshed.
St. George's cross is red to represent bloodshed.
The bottom half of the Polish flag
Is red to represent bloodshed,
While the top half of the Indonesian flag
Is red to represent bloodshed.
The thing every nation has in common is sacrifice.
Our skin of many colours, our blood of only one."

– Day 254

Baijiu Breath

There's a specific kind of morning breath that follows a night on **báijiǔ** (*white alcohol*), and if you've never experienced it, count yourself lucky. Imagine petrol, fermented rice, and revenge. The breath doesn't just sit in your mouth; it seeps from your pores. You wake up feeling like you've been embalmed in ethanol. And yet, I look back on those nights with an odd sort of affection.

The first time I drank baijiu was at a party in the countryside, on a family friend's mountaintop terrace surrounded by mist and the occasional distant light that ephemerally penetrated it. The view was cinematic—rolling hills, echoes of faraway motorbikes, a sky bruised with stars. It felt like something out of a painting. Until you noticed the animals. Chickens and goats fenced a little too restrictively for comfort, watching us celebrate with a kind of silent disapproval. There was also an Alsatian, who sat about three feet from the table, still and silent. A dog who, given the right command in Chinese, would have ripped my nuts off.

After a while, though, I forgot about all that. We were happy. Giddy, even. The baijiu we drank was called **jiǎngxiǎobái** (literally, *river small white*, or more poetically, *the little white of the river*). It was Chongqing's answer to Grey Goose, except it was

60% proof and made from sorghum. It didn't taste good. It tasted like paint stripper, followed by fireworks. But it did the job, and the job was to remove our social anxieties. Everyone became a better dancer. A better singer. I became, without question, a better Mandarin speaker.

There's something about alcohol that makes you forget to be embarrassed. So instead of calculating tones in my head, I just let them out, and people actually understood me. Or at least they nodded and laughed like I did. Either way, it worked. My word-order may have fallen apart, but the joy was mutual.

Interestingly, it's the *men* in China who go to the bathroom in groups. At least, in my experience. All of them. At once. It was the first time I'd seen eight grown men head off together to urinate and smoke in unison. It was like some weird form of synchronised bonding. I remember one night, the father of the family I was staying with—normally shy—offered me a cigarette mid-stream with a goofy smile from behind his thick-rimmed glasses.

What struck me most about Chinese drinking culture was its wholesomeness. People didn't get lairy. No one was shouting or punching hand-driers off walls (which I'd seen more than once in the UK). Instead, people clinked glasses at rotating banquet tables that seated fifty people (and I swear, that's not the baijiu talking. Literally fifty people). They became merrier and more affectionate as the evening went on. Grandfathers would toast you. Strangers would insist you try their province's special dish, or their favourite local **píjiǔ** (*beer*). And everyone, and I mean *everyone*, before every single drink, without fail, would say the word **gānbēi** (*cheers.* Literally: *dry the cup*).

The beer, by the way, was genuinely good. Light, fresh, and always cold. The wine, on the other hand, was tragic. Sharp, synthetic, and often sweetened like cough syrup. I poured myself one glass and thought, *the only thing about this that resembles wine is the shape of the bottle.*

My first night out alone in China involved baijiu too. I'd been feeling restless, curious. I messaged a group of expats I'd met earlier that week—two German lads and an Irish girl, who were in China, I suppose, for familiar reasons. We met on a certain block of Jiefangbei, the neon-lit party district that never seemed to sleep.

The clubs were vast, cathedral-like, with walls that pulsed and speakers that threatened to realign your skeleton. Within twenty minutes, I'd lost the expats completely. Then, just as I was considering calling it a night, I was summoned by a group of rich, Chinese twenty-something-year-olds to join their private booth. They had a bottle of baijiu the size of a fire extinguisher. I don't remember their names, but I remember the buzz, the friendliness, the insistence that I **gānbēi** again and again. It was my first time being invited in like that—like I was more than just a foreign curiosity, but a part of the evening. As far as I could tell, the kaleidoscopic club lighting obscured my skin colour, and the volume level made it impossible for them to hear my (at the time) poor Chinese.

The taxi ride home was the best part of the night. It was 5 a.m., and believe it or not, I was stone-cold sober by then. We were coasting over one of Chongqing's many winding bridges, with the great river below and the skyline twinkling like a city made of constellations. The driver and I chatted in a strange medley of English and Chinese (known colloquially as *Chinglish*), and I felt like the whole world had opened up. The ride lasted over an hour, through tunnels, along riverbanks, over sleeping yet soon-to-be-wide-awake markets. The whole ride cost the equivalent of about a fiver. I paid double and told him to keep the change. He grinned. I grinned. The city was mine. To this day, that taxi ride is one of my most vivid and happiest memories.

That's what baijiu nights were like. Part poetry, part indigestion. Part linguistic breakthrough, part identity crisis. The memories are all a little blurred at the edges—but warm, not painful. And when the breath fades, the stories remain.

"idk where im fell off bed. its the friens
house with the chickens. Had some baiii ju.
CHICKIN OUTSIDE SO LOUD
outsid the wind ow. Bkawwwk."

– Day 85

The Yangtze

I remember standing on the banks of the Mississippi River. I saw it from rural Louisiana, from Natchez, from Baton Rouge, and from old New Orleans. I remember thinking, *this is big*. To anyone who has never touched the Mississippi, the following blues lyrics from a 1934 record by Big Bill Broonzy may sound playful, jolly, and bright:

"Mississippi River
Is so long, deep and wide
I can see my girl
Standin' on that other side."

But when you listen to those words again, with your feet sinking into the great river, you realise the lyrics to that century-year-old song are mournful, not playful. They are sorrowful, not jolly. They are *blue*, not bright. Why? Because the "long, deep and wide" river is a true abuttal of space and time. The girl on that other side is a girl slipping away into the romantic, pitiful past, or at least, slipping away into a future. A future without *you* in it.

As Bill says, the Mississippi River isn't just deep and wide; it's long. And you don't measure it in litres or gallons, or in miles or kilometres. You measure it in centuries. You measure it in history, in heartbreak, in blood, in tears, and in memories. The Mississippi River is the fourth longest in the world.

The Yangtze River is the third.

The Yangtze is a different kind of beast. If the Mississippi is a fresh-water buffalo trail, then the Yangtze is a Chinese dragon, colossal, scaly, sinuous, and all-consuming. The Mississippi is a million little souls. The Yangtze is one giant soul.

In Chongqing, two rivers meet: the vagrant, verdant Jialing, and of course, the brown, broad Yangtze. If the Jialing is a polite suggestion, the Yangtze is a full-body shove. I stood at the confluence once, just upstream of the Chaotianmen docks, and watched the two rivers collide like awkward co-workers forced to share a desk. For a moment, they run side by side: green, brown, green, brown. Then the brown takes over, devouring its green prey.

It isn't subtle. The Yangtze doesn't do subtle. It's a show-off, a know-it-all, a river with elbows. The name in Chinese is **cháng jiāng** (*long river*). Long River, indeed. It runs nigh on four thousand miles from the Tibetan Plateau to the East China Sea, carving through mountain ranges, cities, farmland, and history, like it owns the place. Because in a way, it does.

I've always been fascinated by rivers. Where there is water, there is a story. In fact, stories live and die with them. People have lived along the Yangtze for tens of thousands of years. They have planted rice in its soil, written poetry to its rhythm, and prayed to it when it rose too high. Whole dynasties built their fortunes on what floated down it—rice, silk, porcelain. It's been a trade route, a flood hazard, a metaphor. Whatever. You name it. It's been there and done that.

The Grand Canal connected the Yangtze to the Yellow River—turning it into an inland shipping lane—long before DHL existed. In the Tang and Song dynasties, if you wanted to move goods, ideas, or armies, you used the Yangtze. If you wanted to flee from a battle, you used the Yangtze. If you wanted to write a sad poem about your exile, you probably mentioned the Yangtze. The river has always been there. Through all of it. Mongol invasions. Imperial tax collectors. Floating opera boats. Then, in 1931, one of the worst floods in recorded history killed millions. In the 2000s, the Three Gorges Dam displaced over a million people and submerged entire towns. Ask a local and they'll tell you: You don't mess with the Yangtze. The Yangtze is a god.

I went on a river cruise with some other foreigners one night. We boarded at Chaotianmen, where vendors sold skewers and fake Louis Vuitton bags, and we climbed to the top deck of a boat lit up like a Christmas tree.

Chongqing is not shy about lighting. Bridges glow fuchsia. Skyscrapers display full-screen videos. Lovers send each other's names up to the tallest to have them light up the city, followed by a "<3." Even the water taxis have neon rims. As we sailed down the Yangtze, the skyline didn't just shine—it shouted. The boat glided past towers with names like *Poly Skyline* and *International Finance Plaza*, all reflected in the water like a fever dream.

I leaned over the railing with my cup of lukewarm watermelon juice and thought, *this river has seen emperors, floods, dynasties, and now it sees this*. Somewhere down there, in the inky water, was the ghost of a king. And above it, we were taking selfies.

You can't write about the Yangtze without talking about the fish. There used to be hundreds of species. Paddlefish. River dolphins. Sturgeon. Now, not so much. Overfishing, pollution, and damming have taken their toll. But locals still fish in it. I once ate 'Yangtze fish with pickled greens' in a hot pot place where the waitress wore a panda headband and the menu wore no English. Actually, there was no menu, which was pretty common. The fish was oily, bony, and absolutely delicious.

People still rely on this river. Farmers, ferrymen, seafood vendors. It gives. But it also takes. Floods are less frequent now, thanks to damming, but the cost—ecological and cultural—is still debated over green tea in university lounges.

Rivers have moods, and the Yangtze's is complex. Some days it's calm and glassy, making the city feel almost peaceful. Other days it churns, and stinks, and rises, reminding you who's in charge. Locals walk along its banks at all hours—grandparents doing calisthenics at sunrise, teenagers vaping at midnight. It's a background character in every story, always present, always watching.

I once saw a wedding shoot by the river. The bride was standing in stilettos on a damp stone embankment, clinging to her groom while a photographer shouted instructions. Behind her, the brown water sloshed. It felt like the river could swallow her dress in one gulp, but she smiled anyway. That's the relationship people here have with the Yangtze: wary affection.

By the time I left Chongqing, I'd walked along its banks more times than I could count. I'd seen fishermen in conical hats, businessmen on morning jogs, kids chucking rocks into the water. I'd seen a thousand vertiginous bridges and boats riding so low I wondered how they didn't sink.

There's an old Chinese saying: "If you live near the mountain, live off the mountain; if you live near the water, live off the water." It sounds better in Chinese, but you get the sentiment. The Yangtze has fed millions. It's also swallowed homes, and with them, dreams. I believe you could taste them were you to drink from it... along with pollution.

"Today I looked into the river
And was fascinated by it.
Then the river looked at me,
Got bored, and moved on."

– Day 61

Comedy, Drama, and Propaganda

Wanda Plaza is the English name for a chain of enormous commercial complexes across China. In other words, the few triumphant and awe-inspiring mega-malls in the UK (Westfield, Meadowhall, Trafford Centre, The Bull Ring), to which shoppers journey from all across the country—well, there are about two hundred of them in China... *per city.* Wanda Plaza is just one such conglomerate.

Anyway, the focus of this chapter is not Wanda Plaza, but the cinema, which you find, if I remember correctly, on the third or fourth floor of most of these malls. The cinema itself was nothing special in comparison to Western movie theatres. (Although I'd never sat on a chair that moved in synch with the movie before.) What I really want to talk about here is the movies themselves.

Once a week, or at least once a fortnight, my family would take me to the cinema. It was something of a ritual for many people in China. Apart from on special occasions, the grandparents would stay at home. Usually, it was me, the mum, the dad, the toddler (if appropriate), the teenager, the neighbours, and an aunt or uncle thrown in here and there.

Incidentally, the neighbour's attractive, me-aged daughter would usually sit right next to me, which I would often tell myself constituted a date. In retrospect, it didn't. But more on that later.

The films we watched varied, but they followed a few broad themes: national pride, heroic sacrifice, and making sure everyone knew China was the best country on Earth, and as far as I could tell at the time, the audience was in full agreement.

One night, we watched *The Captain*, a dramatisation of a real-life emergency landing in which a Chinese pilot pulled a Sully Sullenberger with extra turbulence and a touch more screaming. It was gripping, certainly. But what stayed with me wasn't the near-death experience or the miraculous landing—it was the flag-waving at the end, the passengers saluting the flight crew like they'd just won a war. It was the kind of movie where no one has personal flaws, unless that flaw is insufficient patriotism, which they, of course, overcome by the final act. For you see, in a Chinese story, *that* is true character development.

Another time, we saw *The Bravest*, a film about firefighters tackling an oil refinery inferno. It had all the right ingredients: fireballs, sacrifice, sweat dripping into ash-covered brows. I overheated just watching it. But again, it wasn't really about the fire, was it? It was about the country. The real hero of the story, despite all the flames, was the motherland, watching silently over her devoted sons as they died in her service.

Then came *The Climbers*, which follows a team of Chinese mountaineers scaling Everest—sorry, *Mount Qomolangma*, as the film reminded us—and planting the national flag squarely at the top, despite every conceivable meteorological objection. It was a terrific film, without a doubt, and I'd watch it again. Cinematographic and editorial genius. However, it also seemed rather invested in proving that the mountain belonged, administratively and possibly *spiritually*, to China.

But the most memorable, the one that gave me a slightly numb feeling in my fingertips as the credits rolled, was *My People, My Country*, a sweeping anthology of seven mini-stories by various directors, released to mark the 70th anniversary of the founding of the People's Republic. Every story was rooted in a real historical event, from the 2008 Summer Olympics to the construction of China's first atomic bomb. An engineer has a nervous breakdown as he grinds, sleep-deprived, to perfect an automatic flag-hoisting mechanism in time for the 1949 Founding Ceremony. An executive delegate faces enormous pressure to correctly time the 1997 handover of Hong Kong, navigating the twelve-second gap between the lowering of the British flag and the raising of the Chinese flag. There are many fireworks. There are many tears. There is only really one message.

Again, and I hate to admit it, but the movie was bloody phenomenal. Everyone in the cinema cheered and clapped. Like, when do you see that in the West these days? Not since 1955. I clapped too, but more out of social obligation than genuine fervour. Which, in a room full of emotionally overwhelmed patriots, felt like a betrayal. It's easy to get swept up in it, especially when everyone around you is wiping their eyes and humming the national anthem on their way back down the escalator. But something about it made me squirm. It felt like an emotional transaction that I hadn't consented to. I felt like the movie posters with the vetted Chinese actors were watching me. I felt an immense pressure from every angle.

Just a few days later, it was October 1st—China's National Day—and the 70th anniversary of the People's Republic. The streets were awash with red. Children waved flags, adults wore them, buildings were dressed in them. It was less a celebration than a declaration: *We are powerful. We are united. We are watching.* And perhaps most strikingly, everyone—*everyone* as far as I was concerned—tuned in to watch the military parade.

The streets were empty.

This was no Great British fly-past with a couple of Red Arrows and some pensioners playing trumpets. This was a full-scale spectacle: tanks rolling in perfect formation, missiles the size of small office buildings, soldiers with expressions so identical it felt like they'd been copy-pasted into reality. Every segment ended with thunderous applause and that same oddly robotic wave. It was impressive. It was intimidating. It was surreal.

I sat on the sofa with my host family, watching as jet planes formed hearts in the sky. The grandma beamed. The toddler clapped. Even the aloof teenager, the would-be rebel, watched intently from the arm of the sofa. I smiled politely, unsure how to react. I'd never felt so aware of being foreign.

What I found most unsettling wasn't the military might itself—any remotely powerful country loves to flex now and then. It was the unspoken assumption that to be Chinese was to be proud of all this, without question. That there was no room for uncertainty, no possibility that any of this could ever be problematic. Criticism didn't exist. Or if it did, it had the good sense to keep its mouth shut.

In the West, patriotism is, in a lot of circles, discouraged. It is unfashionable. We all question authority, and rightly so. Many detest and excoriate their own country. And that's totally fine. I get it. I really do. There are many things to be critical of. We point out our hypocrisies, our political divisions, our history of violence and conquest. Good. But that criticism exists because we have the freedom to make it. In a cinema in Britain, you can watch a film that tears your own government apart. You can mock your leaders on prime-time television. You can, if you want, write a book about how messed up everything is and have it published and sold without worrying about being followed home.

In China, you can't. Try making a film about government corruption, or military overreach, or even just a character who's not unshakably patriotic, and see how far it gets you. Spoiler alert: It won't. This book, for example—this very one you're reading—would almost certainly be banned in China, and ironically, if it ever sells enough copies in the West, it probably *will* be banned in China. Not because it's dangerous, or inflammatory, or even particularly important. But because it dares to observe without worshipping.

And for that—for the fact that I can sit here and write this, and publish it, and (with any luck) have someone read it—I'm grateful.

Movie nights in China were a bonding ritual. They were a chance to eat popcorn, to sit in massage chairs that tried to eject you during intense scenes, and to feel, for two hours, like you were part of something bigger. That's powerful. But it's also dangerous when that something bigger doesn't allow room for nuance.

"Comedy, action, drama... I've found a new
Genre of film—Propaganda."

– Day 191

The Neighbour's Daughter

Let me just clear something up before I begin: At the time, I was *also* eighteen years old. In fact, the girl in question was three months older than me. And as I write this, I'm currently twenty-four years old and have the most amazing girlfriend in the world. (No, she didn't make me say that.) This chapter is purely reflective. I am simply peering back into my notebook of love, from before I knew what love was.

Of course, this chapter has wider implications than one particular girl in China, but I believe the macro can only be dealt with on the micro, and the national can only be interpreted through the local. In other words, first tackle the day-to-day details, and then bother with the bigger picture. And in this particular quotidian existence, I had a little crush on the girl next door.

How many details do you want? Pretty. Singer. Smiley. And she had my favourite quality of all: *Liking me back.* At least, I am pretty sure she liked me back. She wanted to hang out with me whenever she had the chance, which was not very often since she was either revising, getting ready for university, performing on a stage, or off horse riding in the countryside. OK, so she was spoiled as well. But not in the irritating, tantrum-throwing way.

She was spoiled in that she was talented, a bit pampered, and surrounded by people who adored her.

We never kissed. I think that's important to clarify. I'm not sure we even hugged, which is not particularly uncommon in China. And yet I remember those small moments with startling clarity: Walking side by side with two umbrellas in the rain, buying fried squid at a night market, accidentally matching outfits (her pink hoodie and mine, embarrassingly similar). There was even one time she held my wrist as we crossed a busy street, which I took to mean we were basically engaged.

But, in retrospect, nothing ever happened. And that was probably for the best. The honest-to-God truth is I was homesick, and she gave me a sense of home. Not to mention, I was a teenager, so give me a break. But in the end, she was too busy, and I was too foreign, and she moved to America to study at Princeton... so clearly, out of my league in any case.

After she left, I decided to give 'dating' an actual go. Dating in China as a white person is simultaneously the easiest and most stressful thing imaginable.

First, there's the romanticism. Dating in China can be wonderfully old-fashioned. Handwritten notes, long walks under red lanterns, parents involved by date three. Girls might show up to dinner with gifts. Men are expected to pay, always. It's courtship in its purest form, and for a while I found that refreshing.

But then there's the materialism. It's not just that you're judged by your looks, your job, your prospects—that's universal. It's that in China, you might be asked about your salary, your property, and your reproductive goals before you've even ordered the first drink. A friend once told me, "If you don't own a house, don't bother dating a girl in China."

Nevertheless, I tried. I tried to date. I went on a handful, but none of them were successful by any metric. I dated a twenty-eight-year-old doctor (do the maths), which felt like an accomplishment until I realised she was dating me for the same reason people hang decorative maps in their living rooms: aesthetic appeal and bragging rights.

She liked the idea of me more than she liked me. I was a white boy, and that carried social currency. The only thing that would have been better is if I'd had blue eyes and blonde hair—even more exotic, you see. She held my hand *only* in front of her friends. She bought me flowers and had them motorbiked to me while I was standing alone on a bridge, which is to this day, the *only* time I've ever been bought flowers.

I didn't like it.

It was all incredibly 'romantic'—the kind of romantic that looks good in WeChat posts but doesn't feel good in your stomach. We kissed once, awkwardly, like we were doing it on behalf of our respective countries. And then we stopped. I think we both knew it didn't mean anything. She ghosted me a week later and updated her profile picture to a selfie with a Dutch guy. I couldn't help but laugh at the whole thing.

Another girl I met wanted to talk. And I mean exclusively talk. About grammar. I was her conversational trophy, her personal IELTS exam simulator. I once asked if she wanted to go to the park, and she replied, "That's a great idea. Can you explain the difference between 'at' and 'on' again?"

It was less flirtation, more tuition. So I gave up after date two.

At some point, I stopped bothering with dating Chinese girls altogether. It just didn't work for me. Either I was being subtly interrogated for my suitability as a future husband and father of two children—or I was being wheeled out as a language prop, a novelty item, a limited-edition boyfriend for the socials. I acknowledge, of course, that this does not reflect the outlook of *all* Chinese people. Though I will say I've heard very similar things from other foreigners who have tried to date in China.

The only girl I ended up actually dating semi-long-term in China wasn't Chinese. She was Russian. She was smart, kind, and refreshingly unbothered by my ethnicity. She also didn't ask me how much I earned or how many kids I wanted on our first date, which felt like a win. The only downside I can remember is that she was a heavy smoker, such that the smell (and taste) lingered for weeks.

But let's go back to the girl next door.

In the end, she became a friend. A proper one. The kind you can talk to in the evening about tomorrow but not about the *future*, or about how unfair university entrance exams are, or about why your host family is cooking a turtle again. She shared her music with me. She made me feel welcome. She didn't ask anything of me except that I be myself. And for that, she'll always have a little place in my memory. I made many friends in China, and they were all wonderful in their own way, and I consider myself truly lucky in that way.

Admittedly, I forgot about this girl about four years ago, only to re-remember her after watching a movie set in New Jersey, just outside Princeton. I hope she has graduated and is doing well, as I hope all the lovely people I met in China are doing well.

"Roses are red, violets are blue,
But when it comes to China, I ain't got a clue."

– Day 113

The Plastic Stool

There are a few objects that define life in China—not in a grand, ceremonial way, but in the everyday, the unnoticed, the omnipresent. The electric scooter. The rice cooker. The thermos flask filled with hot water. And then there's plastic stools. You don't notice them at first. Then you start seeing them everywhere, like they've been photoshopped into the background of every scene. Street corner? Plastic stool. A game of mahjong outside a shop? Plastic stools, and one upturned as a table. A child getting a haircut on the pavement? Plastic stool.

It's always the same basic design: four legs, hollow, stackable, sometimes with a flower motif stamped into the seat. Cheap, bright, and unapologetically ugly. Pink, lime green, turquoise, maroon. Made from the kind of plastic that seems like it could shatter or last forever, depending on your mood.

But the thing is—they work. Plastic stools are the great equaliser. No one looks cool on one. CEOs and migrant workers, students and teachers, they all end up on these squat, uncomfortable perches at some point. They wobble. They scrape. They squeak. But old, young, rich, or poor, *everyone* is humbled by the plastic stool.

In Chongqing, where the streets snake up hillsides like noodles flung at a wall, plastic stools are particularly vital. You'll find them on pavements with no real edge, on stairs that double as dining areas, beside hot pot stalls, and under bridges. Locals sit and eat spicy vegetables while watching construction workers dig up the road beside them. There's a kind of democratic elegance to it.

They let you eat and socialise anywhere. That's the magic. No need for a restaurant with chairs and tables. A single cook with a cart, a few stools, a folding table—and suddenly you've got a dining room on the side of a mountain. Food courts materialise wherever the traffic slows. You eat, you sweat, you shout out *thanks*, and then you go.

Some of my best meals in China happened on a plastic stool. Once, at 2 a.m., I sat outside a convenience store eating from skewers dipped in spicy oil, next to a middle-aged couple who offered me beer and tissues in equal measure. Another time, I shared a table with a man and his three cats, none of whom seemed especially concerned about hygiene. We talked about train delays. I think. My Mandarin was sketchy then.

But it wasn't just food. The stools showed up at public dances, at impromptu performances, at street chess tournaments, at charity events, at kids' birthday parties. Once I saw a man sitting on one inside a department store, just staring at a wall of TVs. Another time, a group of students was revising for an exam on a plastic table and four mismatched stools outside a McDonald's. It's like someone pressed pause on society and the stools arrived to catch the moment.

They're ugly, yes. They're crude. They're far from ergonomic. They are mass-produced from oil and petrochemicals, probably belched out of some factory in Zhejiang or Guangdong. And yes, they're bad for the environment, which we cannot overlook.

Landfills will one day overflow with them. The plastic stool will outlive us all. They'll likely be here long after the last humans.

But there's also something undeniably human about them. They're a solution to a problem: How do you sit anywhere? You make a stool that costs nothing and weighs nothing. You make something so easy to carry, to store, to replace, that it becomes a part of the infrastructure. The disposable infrastructure of communal life.

In the West, eating is normally an indoor, contained affair. Even fast food has walls and queues and tables with QR codes. In China, the line between private and public is blurrier. Your dinner table might be a square, a circle, or a cardboard box on the kerb. Your seat might be a plastic stool that's seen a hundred arses before yours. And somehow, it doesn't matter. The experience is still yours.

Plastic stools are a metaphor, too, for a kind of pragmatic collectivism. You don't need comfort to be together. You just need a surface to sit on. They remind you that cities are made not just by architects and planners but by the people who squat, chat, eat, argue, and laugh on them.

Now, back home, I sometimes find myself standing awkwardly at outdoor events, holding a plate of food with nowhere to sit. I think of the stool. How ridiculous it is. How terrible. How perfect.

"In England, this would never do.
Too plastic, too frail, too ugly.
But then in England, we'd have just stayed indoors."

– Day 72

Outside Country Person

In China, one of the most common phrases uttered, at least when I was in the room, was **wài guó rén**. (The literal meaning is *outside country person.*) It means *foreigner.* In China, especially in the parts that don't see many tourists, which at the time, was Chongqing all over, there's a strange and irreversible transformation that happens the moment you step outside: You are no longer just a person. You are a **wài guó rén**. A foreigner. Not a person. Not even a Brit, not even an expat. You are a walking *other.*

In the mornings, on the way to class or a tutoring job, I'd be stared at with the kind of intensity usually reserved for celebrities or natural disasters. People wouldn't usually hide it either. You're sitting on the subway, headphones in, half-asleep, and you feel a gentle, insistent poking at your arm. You open your eyes to find an old lady poking the hair on your forearm, looking amazed, rubbing your skin to see if it's real, or if the 'paint' peels off. Meanwhile, a girl the other side of the train would watch, giggling from behind a fan. I once had a little boy try to unzip my jacket because he wanted to see what a foreigner's *heart* looked like. I still don't really know what he was expecting to see there.

Sometimes they just shout it: **"wài guó rén!"** And suddenly, everyone in a five-metre radius is looking. You're a flash of something different in their day. Whether you like it or not, you're basically YouTube content.

There is a kind of hospitality that comes with it, yes. People are warm, curious, and generous. I was invited to meals by total strangers more times than I can count. At least once a week, someone would insist on buying me a drink or helping me carry something. They would ask for a selfie. There is a kind of pride, too, in hosting a **wài guó rén**, even if you didn't ask to be hosted. That part is lovely. I won't pretend otherwise.

But there's something underneath it too, something that gets to you after a while. You are never *not* a foreigner. You don't get to just be a person. Even when your Mandarin gets good, even when you know how to haggle at the market or how to use chopsticks properly, or how to order food like a local—**wài guó rén** sticks to you like cigarette smoke. You'll always be outside the glass.

And I was lucky. I was white. Which, in China, whether we like it or not, is a kind of currency. It opens doors. It gets you jobs you're not qualified for. It gets you *credibility* in weird ways. But it also comes with its own set of uncomfortable expectations—like being rich, promiscuous, overly friendly, and somehow educated and stupid at the same time. 'White monkey jobs' are a whole industry, where you get hired just to *look foreign* in a brochure or at a business dinner.

But that's nothing compared to what my Black friends went through. Suspicion. Avoidance. Rude comments. I remember one guy from Kenya who told me he was asked once, by a stranger in the park, if he was a criminal. Just like that. Not out of hate, not even really out of malice—just ignorance, dressed up as curiosity.

And the most surreal part? They'd often talk *to* me *about* other foreigners, as if I weren't one. "You know, foreigners don't understand Chinese culture," someone would say to me at a dinner table, chopping duck with a cleaver, while I sat there with my chopsticks, wondering if I should agree or not. "Foreigners don't know how to count." "Foreigners don't eat spicy food." "Foreigners don't understand respect like we do."

"Interesting," I'd say. "Tell me more."

Of course, I'm generalising about generalising. I know that. Not everyone in China treated me that way. Some people forgot I was foreign five minutes after we started talking. Some didn't care at all. In a country of 1.4 billion people, there are always contradictions, always exceptions.

But still—it wears on you. It's a kind of soft alienation that doesn't hurt at first but builds slowly. Being the **wài guó rén** is like wearing a birthday hat. At first, it's funny, then it's attention-grabbing, then soon, it's just annoying, and you want to throw it in the bin.

Every day was a performance. Every day, I was either a clown or a guest of honour. Sometimes both.

I had one friend who loved the attention. Tall, blond, loud. He leaned into it, taught kids how to shout English phrases like, "You're the best teacher in the world!"

"Who's the best teacher in the world?"

"You are!"

But even he, after a few months, confessed that he was tired of it. "I just want to go somewhere where no one notices me," he said. "Where I can go buy noodles and no one points."

And still, there was kindness. So much kindness. It's a strange thing, being constantly othered and constantly welcomed at the same time. You learn to navigate the tension. You learn which smiles are real and which ones are performative. You start to understand when a compliment is just etiquette, and when someone is genuinely glad to see you.

Some of the best conversations I had in China were about this very topic. Chinese friends who asked me what racism looked like in the West, which is something they'd heard about on the news but didn't understand. They wanted to know what it was like to live in a country with people from all around the world.

But I never stopped being **wài guó rén**. Even when I was fluent enough to argue with salesmen or explain the basic plot of British TV shows. Even when I was defending China to Westerners who didn't understand it. Still, the label remained.

There was one moment that summed it up. I was on a packed bus one morning, and an old man offered me his seat. I tried to refuse, but he insisted. "You're a foreigner," he said with a warm smile. "We like foreigners."

Those two sentences stayed with me. You're a foreigner. We like foreigners. It means I like you, but you are a guest, and it is because you are a guest that I like you.

It's not that being a **wài guó rén** is bad. It's just that it's... lonely. You make thirty-five new friends a day, but they're not *your people*. Not really. Not yet. You're exotic, interesting, novel. But not familiar. Not *home*. And the oddest part of all? When I came back to the UK, I missed it. I missed being *visible*. I missed the curiosity, the accidental fame. I missed the feeling that every stroll down the street might end in an unexpected conversation or invitation. At home, I was just another face in the crowd, which is probably how Chinese people feel in *China*. But there's no equivalent for them. In the West, especially in the UK, we already have the world on our doorstep. In this way, **wài guó rén** really is a unique phenomenon.

Sometimes I think the hardest part of being a **wài guó rén** is not the isolation or the stereotypes, but the fact that, in some strange and permanent way, you lose your invisibility. And once it's gone, you're never quite sure if you want it back. Being **wài guó rén** brought me a thousand experiences that I would never have otherwise known, but among those experiences were ones that made me look hard at what exactly I meant in a world that was not mine.

"I'm either a celebrity or a zoo animal.
Maybe one is not so different from the other."

– Day 38

The True Meaning of 1,400,000,000

There are 1.4 billion people in China.

Let me say that again: There are 1,400,000,000 people in China.

No, that's still just a figure on a page. It fails to demonstrate just how big that number is. What if I wrote 1.4 billion words out for you individually? Well, if I typed 1.4 billion words, assuming I averaged two thousand words a day and didn't stop until I'd finished, it would take me *two thousand years* to finish.

1.4 billion people! It's not a side-note or an interesting statistic. It is *the* statistic. It is the ghost behind every queue. It is the reason you can't find a quiet bench anywhere. It is a number so absurdly large that it stops meaning anything after a while—until you live in it.

When you first arrive in China, it feels like everyone is everywhere, all at once. You get on a train and it's full. You try to cross the road, and the pedestrian crossing is more of a group migration. You go to a park for some quiet reflection and find yourself in the middle of a line-dancing club, a kite battle, and a game of volleyball. And it's not that these people are being inconsiderate. It's just that there are... so many of them.

I remember visiting a supposedly peaceful mountain temple and having to queue for twenty minutes just to get my photo next to the entrance. I remember rush hour on the metro, where the doors would open and nobody could get off or on because the density had reached critical mass.

This population clustering explains a lot. It explains why cities are so vertical—you've got to stack people like pancakes. It even explains why getting a table at a restaurant on a Tuesday night sometimes requires the strategic cunning of a chess grandmaster.

Here's something you might not know: Despite China being one of the largest countries in the world by landmass, most of it is virtually uninhabited. The vast majority of the population—over 90%, in fact—live in the eastern third of the country. Imagine drawing a squiggly line from the top-right corner of the map down to the bottom-left. That bit on the right? Teeming with people. The rest? Mountains, deserts, high-altitude wilderness, and goats.

As it happens, Chongqing is one of the few major cities that bucks the trend. It sits inland, closer to the geographic centre than the coastline, surrounded by mountains and mist, and yet it has a population of over thirty million in its greater metropolitan area. That's more than the entire population of Australia. And for a city that's not even on most Westerners' radar, that should give you an idea of the scale we're dealing with here.

So, what do you do when your population gets too big? If you're China in the late 20th century, you impose one of the most controversial social engineering policies in modern history: *The One Child Policy*.

Introduced in 1980, the One Child Policy was a response to fears that unchecked population growth would strain resources, increase poverty, and destabilise the nation's economic progress, which, to be fair, were not completely irrational fears. China was emerging from a century of turmoil—colonialism, civil war, famine, the Cultural Revolution—and the government saw demographic control as essential to national recovery.

But the execution of the policy was—there's no way around it—utterly brutal. Families who defied the rule could face fines, job loss, and even forced sterilisation. Certain areas had slightly more flexibility, sometimes being allowed a second child if the first was a girl or disabled. But in most cities, the rule of one was rigid. Many women were coerced into abortions. Children born 'illegally' were often denied **hù kǒu** (*household registration*), which meant they had no access to education, healthcare, or legal employment.

There's no official number for how many abortions were performed under duress. There's no official number for how many children were born undocumented, or given away, or abandoned. But the numbers we do have are chilling.

And then there's the gender imbalance. Because of longstanding cultural preferences for sons (generally speaking), the policy led to sex-selective abortions and female infanticide on a scale that distorted the population. Today, there are millions more men than women in China. Whole generations of young men, especially in rural areas, have no hope of finding a partner, which leads to all sorts of other social issues, from loneliness and depression to, in some cases, the rise of human trafficking.

The *One Child Policy* was replaced by a *Two Child Policy* in 2016, and then a *Three Child Policy* in 2021, after it became clear that the very problem it was designed to fix had been inverted into a new, inside-out version of the same problem.

In 2022, China's population peaked. For the first time in decades, the number began to decline. And according to most projections, this trend was not just a blip—it was a cliff edge. China is on track to lose hundreds of millions of people over the next century, with some estimates suggesting the population could halve by 2100.

The reasons are familiar: urbanisation, education, career prioritisation, housing costs, and general existential fatigue—in other words, the same reasons people in the West are having fewer kids—except here it's compounded by decades of state-enforced reproductive control. Raising a child in a Chinese city is expensive. Daycare, schooling, extracurriculars, housing—it's all geared toward intense academic and social competition. And many young couples just don't want to put themselves (or a child) through it.

So now the government is encouraging people to have more kids. There are financial incentives. Extra maternity leave. Propaganda posters showing happy families of five. But it's hard to reverse decades of messaging that taught people children were a burden. I saw it in some of the young people I met in China, a kind of quiet resentment for the pressure their own parents put on them, and a determination not to repeat the cycle. And then, in a full-circle twist, you have grandparents practically begging their adult children to reproduce, while those same children are like, "Yeah, maybe after I buy a flat, start a business, retire, and finish therapy."

One thing you come to realise in China is that scale is both a blessing and a curse. You can build a train network that spans the entire country. You can manufacture enough laptops for the planet. But you can also lose people. Not just statistically—emotionally, relationally. In a system that must manage 1.4 billion lives, individuality becomes a logistical inconvenience.

That's not to say people don't matter. They do. I met so many warm, generous, thoughtful individuals in China. But it's easy to see how someone might start to feel small. Interchangeable. Replaceable. Especially if you're poor. Or a woman. Or unregistered. Or just unlucky.

Since my mum was born, the world population has more than doubled. Her mum saw the world population *quadruple* in her lifetime. I hear these generations complaining about the state of the world, and most of the time it is blamed on the amount of people in it—and that's fair—but the people who complain the most about the world population are often those most appalled by drastic measures like the one employed in China.

There's an old saying: In the West, you're a person first and a citizen second. In China, you're a citizen first, and a person second. I don't know if that's entirely fair, but I do know that whenever I tried to imagine what it would be like to grow up in a place where your birth itself was a potential crime, it made me feel a little sick.

Sometimes, in the early morning, I'd look out from the balcony of my host family's apartment. Dozens of windows lit up. Figures moving behind curtains. Mothers prepping breakfast. Fathers ironing shirts. Teenagers scrolling through their phones with one eye open. Old people stretching. The city waking up. And I'd think: This is what 1.4 billion people looks like. Not a number. Not a problem, necessarily. *Certainly* not a solution. Just people. And I'm lucky to be here among them.

"Somewhere in the world, a baby is born every second,
And not a single one of them can be blamed for
The evils and failures of the world.
They just got here."

– Day 185

The Squat Toilet

The first time I used a toilet in China, I wasn't emotionally prepared. There was no soft entry point to this experience. No gentle transition from your familiar world of knee-high, arse-supporting seats and double-ply toilet paper into what I can only describe as *The Porcelain Abyss*—an abyss that demanded no short amount of humility, and above all, flexibility.

It was not until my second day in China that I finally visited a toilet. I went to visit the agency that had sponsored my visa, but I had to make a little stop along the way. When I entered the public facilities, I was confronted with a tiled stall containing nothing but a hole in the floor, a flusher mechanism I didn't recognise, and a wet floor that suggested recent activity (or a leak).

There was also no toilet paper. Not even the carcass of a cardboard tube. Just a small sign that said, in Chinese, *Must bring your own toilet paper.* In hindsight, that was unusual. Normally, there *was* no sign. It was just a given thing that you carried toilet paper with you wherever you went.

Now, let me be clear: The squat toilet is not some underdeveloped prototype. It is not a failed version of the *real thing*, and it's not what some might call 'third world.' In many ways, it's *better* than Western toilets. It's cleaner thanks to a lack of skin-to-seat contact. It's healthier—less strain on the colon, apparently. It's even more water-efficient, supposedly.

If you grow up with squat toilets, they're second nature—fast, hygienic, efficient. But when you *don't* grow up with them? It's a different story. It's like stepping into a boxing ring of the wrong weight class. There's a technique to it. You've got to line yourself up, squat all the way down, and maintain balance while conducting delicate operations. This is especially challenging if you're wearing a backpack. Or a long coat. Or trousers with a complicated button system.

The first time, I panicked. Not because of the physical gymnastics, but because of the mental gymnastics. Every second was filled with doubt: *Am I going to fall in? What if I drop my phone? What if this is how I die? Is this really how I want to be remembered?*

Somewhere between squatting and sweating, I had an epiphany: This wasn't just about toilets. This was about adaptation. About discomfort. About the silent rules of another society, gently reminding me that I was no longer on my own turf.

Western toilets coddle you. They're padded, elevated thrones that give you a break, a seat, a sense of dignity. They're private, sometimes even accompanied by background music and air fresheners. Some of them feel closer to small reading rooms than waste disposal units.

But squat toilets ask something more ancient and primal of you. They don't pamper. They demand. They say, *you were born with knees, use them.* They bring you back down to Earth, so to speak.

There's also no room for lingering. You do your business and get out. Forget about magazines, newspapers, or phone screens.

Forget about doomscrolling. Just in, out, done. Efficient. Transactional. Like most public interactions in China.

And maybe that's what struck me: In many parts of Chinese society, especially in public, efficiency is prized over comfort. There's a kind of collective agreement that practicality comes first. Whether it's toilets, train systems, or bureaucracy, the goal is output. Keep the line moving. Don't waste time. There's very little fuss. No one is standing around waiting for luxury. They have brought their own toilet paper, they are used to squatting, and they have already disappeared back into the crowd before you've even figured out how to flush.

There was a time I visited a *rural* toilet. Different thing altogether. That's like *next-level* China, as if it were a video game and you decided to set the difficulty to 'hard.' There I discovered the toilets were just open troughs, separated by low walls—no doors. You squatted in full view of the next person. The smell was biblical. I tried to wait it out, then gave up and sprinted in, eyes down, dignity left at the entrance like shoes in a sacred temple.

There were plenty of mishaps that year. I've redacted the details—I think as a legal requirement. But over time, I got used to these squatters. I even came to respect them. Not love, exactly, but appreciate. In the same way, you come to appreciate a cold shower or a steep hike.

The toilets taught me something else, too: Everyone is equal when squatting. There's no status in that position. No power pose. Just knees bent, eyes down, doing something deeply human. It's hard to feel superior when your pants are around your ankles and you're aiming for a hole in the floor. In a society with rigid hierarchies, unspoken rules, and face-saving rituals, the squat toilet is quietly democratic. No one escapes it. CEOs, farmers, teachers, tourists—we all squat the same.

And maybe that's part of why they endure. Not just for hygiene or habit, but because they strip you down—literally and metaphorically—to your most human self. It connects you with your roots, with your ancestors. It's practically prehistoric. The modern seated toilet, which we take for granted, didn't become commonplace in the West until the 19th century. Before that, we had bog-houses, holes in the ground, and Mother Nature.

Squatting is older than we are, and so in that sense, China's got it right. In that sense, *we're* the weird ones.

"I visited a toilet today, because I couldn't hold it any longer. Still can't feel my thighs. Adaptation is painful."

– Day 2

Sore Shoulder Blades and Sightlessness

It was about halfway through my time in China. It may have been the bamboo bed. It may have been my exercise-book-heavy backpack. Either way, I needed to relieve the intense ache in my back, so I decided to treat myself to a massage. Besides, in the district of my university accommodation, they were inexpensive. Commonplace. Necessary. Not at all sumptuous. So, I walked into a massage parlour.

I hadn't noticed they were blind at first.

Not in that self-congratulatory, I-don't-see-disability kind of way, but because the whole place was so dimly lit and quiet, it felt like I'd entered a sensory deprivation tank that happened to smell like tiger balm and menthol. The woman at the reception had waved me forward without looking up, muttering something about **tuīná**—a word I'd come to learn meant a specific type of therapeutic massage. But for my purposes, it meant *one part medicine and two parts pain.*

It wasn't until I was led to a room by a middle-aged man who kept one hand brushing the wall and the other outstretched in front of him that I realised: They were blind. All of them. I walked into a room of three men, three women, and a cat, and I was the only 'seeing' one in there. Yes, they had even adopted a blind stray cat.

The man who worked on me was probably in his fifties. He had hands like old river stones: rounded and worn, but strong. He didn't speak except to check once—**zhèlǐ kěyǐ ma?** (*Is this okay here?*) And I replied, a little too quickly, **kěyǐ kěyǐ**, because I didn't know how to say, "Yes, but also I think you've dislodged one of my kidneys."

There was something disarming about it. In the West, massages (at least the ones I've heard of) are always half-sensual, half-transactional—normally delivered in spas where the receptionist wears dove white, while words like "tension" and "deep tissue" flutter around your head. You always feel slightly embarrassed about your body: too hairy, too dry, too pale, too sweaty, too fat.

But here, none of that mattered. This man didn't know the colour of my skin, for one thing. And he didn't give a damn if I was fat or skinny. All he knew was where the pressure needed to go.

There's a kind of vulnerability to being touched by someone who can't judge you visually. Dare I say *intimate?* It's not romantic, and definitely not erotic. That's not what I mean. It's almost... reverent. They're reading your body like Braille, searching for the sentence that explains why your shoulders feel like concrete and your calves twitch at night. Why you have a headache, why you always feel this inexplicable weight behind your eyes.

I kept wondering to myself about how many bodies this man must have read. Hundreds? Thousands? What patterns had his hands memorised? Were there stories he could tell just from the way someone's spine tilted, or how their jaw locked, or how they cried in pain?

Later, I found out that this wasn't a rare phenomenon. **Mángrén ànmó** (*blind person massage*) is a whole industry in China. Not just tolerated but promoted, celebrated, and held in high regard. It turns out that in the 1950s, the Chinese government began pushing massage therapy as a career path for visually impaired people. At the time, employment opportunities were scarce, and massage, with its emphasis on touch and bodily intuition, was seen as a natural fit.

By now, it's practically institutional. Many schools for the blind teach **tuīná** as part of their curriculum. There are state-run training programs. Some cities even give tax breaks to parlours that employ blind therapists. In a strange way, blindness itself has become a qualification; proof that the practitioner is more sensitive, more in tune, more trustworthy. And it's not just clever marketing, either. The masseur really did fix me. It was painful throughout, but at the end, I felt like I'd been given a new body.

I asked a Chinese colleague about it one day. He shrugged and said, "It's good work. Honest work. Blind people need jobs."

But it felt like more than that.

In the West, disability is often treated as something tragic, or else inspirational in a way that's almost patronising. We make documentaries about blind climbers or deaf musicians and call them heroes. But we rarely build systems that make use of difference as a strength. In China—or at least in this one, narrow slice of it—there seemed to be space for that. Not full inclusion, not utopia. I'm not naïve. I'm sure blind people in China still face massive challenges, especially outside urban centres. But something about **mángrén ànmó** stuck with me. It wasn't about pretending blindness didn't exist. It was about recognising it as a different kind of expertise.

And as I lay there, gritting my teeth through a particularly unforgiving pair of hooked fingers just under my eye-sockets, I realised: This man knew more about me in twenty minutes than many people learned in a month. Not because he could see me, but because he *couldn't*, because he didn't need to.

When the massage was over, I sat up slowly, feeling a bit like a sack of wet laundry. The man stood back, waiting. I thanked him clumsily—**xièxie nǐ**—and he smiled in a way that didn't quite reach his eyes but felt genuine all the same. Perhaps he'd known I was foreign as soon as I walked in—or perhaps he'd just figured it out thanks to my not-so-perfect Mandarin—but my race mattered less to him (and the others in the room) than any other person I'd met so far. After I thanked him, he turned, and with the same practiced ease, tapped his way back down the hallway toward the reception.

I lingered. Not out of fatigue, but because I wanted to stay in that moment a little longer—that space where I was just a body among bodies without clothes, or labels, or pretences.

There's a strange clarity in being unseen. It strips away the performance of self. You stop worrying about how you look and start focusing on how you feel. And maybe that's what made **mángrén ànmó** so memorable—not the soreness in my shoulder blades, but the rare, quiet feeling of being known without being observed. **Xièxie nín**.

"I think, sometimes, I need to see less
And feel more."

– Day 168

The Ghost of Riben

There's a name that floats just beneath the surface of modern-day China, especially among the older and middle-aged generations—a name that can still turn a room's mood to ice, that summons shadows from a past people neither want to remember nor forget. That name is **Rìběn** (*Japan*).

I learned early on that this wasn't just another name for just another country. It came freighted with history, pain, anger, and frankly, hatred. This wasn't the casual dislike people might hold for a rival football team or a noisy neighbour. It was a deep, visceral, national grudge.

"**Rìběn rén hěn è**" (*The Japanese are bad people*).

I heard it so many times, whispered and shouted, sometimes with a kind of sorrowful bitterness that made it impossible to argue with.

"**Rìběn rén shì qiángjié zhě**" (*The Japanese are rapists*).

That phrase, more than any other, stuck with me. It was a blunt, brutal accusation.

"Rìběn rén hěn bàolì" (*The Japanese are violent*).

It wasn't just some vague historical resentment. It was personal. If I met anyone born before 1980, they were sure to have similar opinions. But where does this come from? What makes Japan the eternal enemy in China's collective memory?

The answer lies, as many answers do, in the dark umbra of the 20th century—a time when Imperial Japan invaded, occupied, and devastated large parts of the nation. The scars left by that era are not only visible on buildings and monuments but engraved in family stories and everyday attitudes.

One evening, I was sitting with the grandmother of my host family. She was quiet most of the night, sipping tea and watching the news. I asked her if she had always lived in Chongqing. She told me that, as a young girl, she lived in the Northeast. When I asked about her childhood, her face hardened.

"My village was destroyed by Japanese soldiers," she said, voice low. "They killed many people. My mother hid me under the floorboards."

She looked away, her eyes glossy with memories too painful to fully share. Still, she continued. I should tell you that it took online translation tools and considerable concentration on my part to fully understand what she was divulging. This was complicated and hard-hitting vocabulary. Much of what I ascertained, I feel, should be kept to myself. But I can tell you this: She told me stories of raids, of neighbours disappearing, of brutal acts committed in the name of war.

It is easy to dismiss history as distant, intangible, and even academic. But hearing it from someone who *lived* it made it raw, immediate, and impossible to ignore. I feel a similar way when listening to holocaust survivors.

These people are from a different time. It just so happens that people like me—who were born in the first year of the new century—came to this world at the dawn of a new age, an age built out of the ash of some of humanity's most painful and ferocious fires. By now, most of the ash has blown away in the forgetful winds. It is too easy for my generation to downplay the past, to simplify it, deny it, or simply disregard it, and I fear that this trend will be even more prevalent in the generation that follows mine.

But this grandma—whom I knew only as **wàipó** (*mother's mother*)—was alive and unapologetically well. She wasn't going anywhere anytime soon, and I imagine she will live as a strong and indelible reminder of the past for many years to come.

The war wasn't just a conflict of nations. It was a trauma passed down through generations, retold over dinner tables, lamented in schools, and cited in parliamentary buildings. And sometimes, it felt like it was more than just history. It was a warning, a scar, a grievance that shaped how many Chinese people viewed Japan, even today.

But then I wondered: Was this hatred unique to China? Or was it something any country would carry for decades after suffering invasion and atrocity?

I thought of Britain, and I thought of Germany.

Britain, of course, fought two world wars against Germany (among other nations). What images come to mind? The Blitz, the Battle of the Atlantic, and the half a million dead—from Britain alone. It was unimaginably horrific. And yet, today, British people seldom speak of Germans as monsters. There's rivalry—football teams, political disagreements—but not the same deep, existential hatred I heard for the Japanese in China.

Why?

One reason might be time. Another might be politics. More than seventy-five years have passed since World War II ended. But so much of China's relationship with Japan is tangled up in its modern identity. The government likes to remind the people where its values come from, and many of these values emerged from the war.

Japan and China's relationship after the war has been fraught, to put it mildly. Political tensions flare up regularly, over disputed islands, trade wars, and historical apologies that feel half-hearted or insincere to many Chinese people.

But perhaps the biggest difference is narrative. In Britain, the story we tell ourselves about Germany is one of redemption, peace, and reconciliation. We focus on how the future was built—not just on what was lost. In China, the narrative around Japan often remains about victimhood and injustice. The ghosts of the past still haunt the present.

And that's not always a bad thing, as I've said. Remembering history, no matter how painful, is crucial. But it can also trap people in cycles of anger, suspicion, and stereotyping.

I heard stories that left me unsettled. Older people telling me that the Japanese were inherently violent or cruel. Young people unsure if their teacher's history lessons exaggerated or glossed over the truth. But it wasn't just about Japan. In many parts of China, I found that old ideas persisted, even when they were no longer congruent with the present reality.

There were lingering suspicions about foreigners in general—the **wàiguó rén**—seen as mysterious, privileged, salacious, or dangerous. There were stereotypes about urban versus rural people, about wealth and education, and about what it meant to be 'modern.' Some people clung to outdated notions about women, family honour, and social hierarchy. Some ideas survived in quiet corners of society, while others roared loudly in the news or on social media.

What struck me most was how these outdated ideas coexisted with China's rapid modernisation and technological leaps. Smartphones and high-speed trains sat alongside age-old beliefs.

The ghost of **Rìběn** is a symbol of this tension. It's the reminder that history is never just history. It's living, breathing, and it's shaping how people think, feel, and act. It's the past demanding attention, respect, and sometimes justice. But it's also a challenge—to remember without being trapped, to honor pain without breeding hatred.

The ghost of **Rìběn** is one example of how history shapes identity and perception, but it also raises bigger questions: How do societies deal with trauma? When does memory become myth? How do people move forward when the past still weighs so heavily?

I don't have answers. But I do know that understanding these ghosts, and their origins, and the power they wield is essential to understanding China itself. Because beneath the skyscrapers, the neon lights, and the busy streets, are stories that refuse to be forgotten. Stories that still whisper, still haunt.

"Today, in my little diary, I just want to remember:
There are some very brave men and women
Who came before me, who made my life,
Let alone my journey here,
Possible."

– Day 140

The Sky Way

They call it the **qīngguǐ** (*light rail*), which is pronounced as ching-gway for those of you who are unfamiliar with pinyin. Most of the time, I liked to think of it as the 'Sky Way,' since it kind of rhymed, and since most of the rails were built on top of the city streets. Maybe 'Star Way' would be better. It certainly felt like something out of a sci-fi franchise, accompanied by galactic battles, where I fought to wedge myself out from the armpit of a stranger at rush hour. Either way, the Sky Way became a major character in my life in Chongqing. I loved it. I hated it. But mostly, I was fascinated by it.

The Sky Way is fast. Not just fast in the zippy, Japanese bullet-train sense, but fast in the sense that no matter how far-flung your destination is, you get there in half the time you'd predicted, and with only a mild panic attack about whether you've ended up in the wrong province. It slides in and out of stations like a magician doing sleight-of-hand tricks, so efficiently you barely realise it's already moving again. There's no dilly-dallying. Doors open. People pile in. Doors close.

The views from the Sky Way are stunning. Part of that is down to the fact that Chongqing itself is stunning. It's a vertical jungle of buildings and green spaces climbing hills like drunken Tetris blocks, rivers crisscrossing through the centre, bridges coiling over water like snakes. But the Sky Way gives you a vantage point like no other. It floats above the city, ducking in and out of tunnels, emerging to give you a flash of skyline or a glimpse of the Yangtze. One moment you're burrowing through the belly of a mountain, and the next you're flying above rooftops.

And then, of course, there's *that* stop. The one everyone talks about. The one that goes straight through a block of flats—**lǐzǐbà zhàn**. I remember the first time I passed through it. It was way too intimate. You're inside a building, literally, and can see the backs of people's air conditioners clinging to the wall. I half-expected to see someone brushing their teeth out the window. But no, it's all glass, and concrete, and perfectly planned. A metro line surgically embedded into someone's living room.

The stops along the Sky Way line are like the chapters of a storybook. Each one gives you a slightly different flavour of the city. Each one thickens the plot further. There's Shapingba with its university energy and smoky barbecue stalls. There's Jiefangbei, the glitzy downtown area, where it's all Gucci and LED screens, where you can accidentally spend a month's budget in twenty minutes if you're not careful. Daping is another one—a kind of intermediary zone where older neighbourhoods meet the new. And then there's Yudong (which literally means *fish cave*), where the blue line connects to the green. It sounds like a forgotten fishing village, but it is in fact a bustling suburban zone at the end of the line.

Yudong was one of my favourite stops, though it's hard to explain why. It was where I found peace, just far enough from the buzz of the city to feel like I could breathe. I had a routine: Every Friday, after my daily chores, work, and study, I'd go down to Yudong, just to be on my own for a while by the river.

The station itself was far from glamorous, but it had its charms. There was a lady who sold sweet potatoes out front. There were old men playing Mahjong under a pavilion. There was a fantastic soup restaurant overlooking the river.

Of course, it wasn't all so idyllic. Rush hour on the Sky Way deserved its own horror sub-genre. I once saw a girl pushed out of the train because there simply wasn't room for her body inside. Just—*boop*!—gone. The doors closed, and she stood there like a forgotten extra in a musical. The worst part was that no one batted an eye, not even her mother. It was commonplace, you see.

Getting off at your stop was a skill that required practice. You had to anticipate it three stations in advance, inching toward the doors like you were in a human pinball machine. You apologised a lot. Well, if you were English, you apologised a lot. We like to apologise for all sorts of things. You made yourself small. You developed a sixth sense for when the train was about to accelerate or decelerate, so you could brace against someone's backpack instead of tumbling into a stranger's chest. And when your stop came? You went. You didn't hesitate. You pushed like your life depended on it. I once got off with a shoe missing. It was worth it.

There's a theory I heard from one of the expats—let's call him Conspiracy Dave—that the whole reason China invests so heavily in public transport is to discourage car ownership. Cars represent personal freedom, whereas trains can be monitored, scheduled, and tightly controlled. I can't say whether that's true, but I do seem to recall that owning a car in Chongqing was both inconvenient and unnecessary for the average person, thanks in no small part to the Sky Way. Maybe that's the point. Or maybe it's just because roads in Chongqing twist and loop like spaghetti thrown at a wall, and because no one wants to die driving up a vertical hill in a smoggy rainstorm.

In any case, I thoroughly enjoyed the Sky Way. I loved its perplexing predictability. I loved how a friendly robotic voice would announce each stop in crisp Mandarin: **"Xià yí zhàn, Dàpíng"** (*Next stop, Daping*). I loved the way the doors slid open with that neat *ding*. I loved that I could hop on and go anywhere in the city for less than the price of a single baozi.

Some days I'd ride it for no reason. I'd just sit, watching the buildings float past, the city rolling out like a pop-up book. It was one of the few times in China I could simply be still—not a foreigner performing for curious eyes, not a language learner flailing for vocabulary, not a guest in an unfamiliar rhythm, like a samba dancer trying to perform a waltz. I was just a person on a train, watching a foggy sunset.

I recently looked at a map of the Chongqing 'Sky Way' system. Below, I have noted some of the stops that stood out to me, to which I could attach a handful of memories. It's strange; I can still hear the robotic voice announcing each syllable so clearly. They ring in my ear, years later.

Guangdianyuan - Line 6
Yudong - Line 2/3
Chalukou - Line 3
Nanping - Line 3
Chongqing Technology & Business University - Line 3
Hongqiheguo - Line 6
Linjiangmen - Line 2
Daping - Line 1/2
Bashan - Line 5
Lianglukou - Line 1/3

"There are more metro stops in Chongqing,
than there are days I've so far spent in China."

– Day 177

The Sideways Storm of Sanya

There is a kind of storm that doesn't strike downwards. I'd never seen one before. I'd read about horizontal lightning (or "anvil crawlers," or "spider lightning," if you're feeling poetic). But until that moment, I hadn't realised just how alien something as familiar as lightning could become. They were not bolts from the heavens, not a divine exclamation mark. It was a nervous system twitching across the night sky. A spiderweb of silent rage arching sideways, as though the clouds were arguing amongst themselves and had forgotten about the earth entirely.

The storm was unsure of itself, conflicted and anomalous—I related to that. I was standing barefoot on a beach just outside Sanya, the southernmost city on the Island of Hainan, witnessing the sky's quarrel.

Behind me was the flicker of high-rise hotel windows and the faint sound of karaoke music leaking from a beach bar far enough away to sound like I *might* be imagining it, washed out by the ocean breeze, coughing over my head. Ahead of me: black sea, black sky, occasional white violence. And beneath me: warm, salty water washing over my ankles in the rhythm of a gentle waltz.

That moment was a rare one. I was completely alone on the beach, other than the occasional crab skittering past my feet, not to mention the air wrapping me in ions and salt. It might have been the most peaceful moment of my life in China. Or, at the very least, the clearest. And I don't mean peaceful in the sense of 'relaxed' or 'content.' I mean the kind of peace that arrives uninvited, sits beside you without asking, and doesn't speak. It simply exists with you. It doesn't apologise for your loneliness. It doesn't suggest distractions or solutions. It simply allows you to feel, without analysis.

I was alone in a way that felt cosmic. And it was in that solitude, cradled between the sideways storm and the skittering crabs, that I felt more *connected* than ever before.

I was in Hainan on holiday with my host family. It was one of those big Chinese extended-family holidays where every meal is an event and every decision is a group vote. There were aunties, uncles, and cousins I'd never met. To be perfectly honest with you, I didn't have the faintest idea who half of them were.

Hainan is often referred to as 'China's Hawaii,' which I suppose is fair enough if you ignore the geopolitics and the concrete hotels. It's a tropical island—lush, humid, palm-fringed, and blessed with beaches that curve like calligraphy brushstrokes. Chinese tourists come in droves. Domestic flights arrive by the hour, packed with mainlanders in bucket hats, dragging squeaky suitcases and selfie sticks.

It was hot. A thick, wet heat that makes swimming trunks stick to you in the most uncomfortable sort of way. Whether from the ocean or my own sweat, I was drenched for my entire stay.

My main responsibility on that trip was to look after two of the younger children. The first was the host family's two-and-a-half-year-old boy, who had taken to calling me *Samu,* which is a Chongqingified version of *Shanmu,* which is the Chineseified version of my English name. The second was the family's five-year-old niece, who simply called me **gēge** or *older brother.* She also had a habit of asking me unanswerable questions. Example:

"Gege, where do the fish go when they sleep?"

"Uh, the ocean. They sleep in the ocean."

"I know. But *where* in the ocean?"

Their parents were busy reading books under parasols, sipping coconut milk, and enjoying well-deserved naps. One morning, I was asked—asked is the wrong word, it was more of a gentle nomination—to walk the children along the beach to meet the rest of the family at a water park five miles away.

I blinked.

"You trust me with them?" I asked, startled. "I don't think I can find my *own* way there."

The mum laughed, as if that was a silly question. "Of course," she said. "You are a good brother. Take them. Take them. Go. Go."

Like the Chinese word for 'come here,' the word for 'go' is forceful. Not to be argued with:

> ***Zǒu ba!*** *Normally repeated twice. "Go on!"*
> *And there's the more thorough* ***kuài zǒu****. "Quick go!" (Hurry!)*

We set off in the late morning. The heat was already humming. The boy was clingy. He had a habit of wrapping his whole hand around my thumb and refusing to let go. The girl was more independent, striding ahead like she had somewhere to be, and I was merely holding her back. She collected things as she walked—shells, driftwood, bottle caps. She tried to catch a crab and then lost interest mid-chase.

I found myself teaching again. Not just words in English, though there was plenty of opportunity for that: *coconut, sand, sun.* But also things I'd learned as a child. When we reached the roads, I taught them to look both ways. I showed them how to skim stones. The boy tried but ended up just throwing pebbles directly at his own feet. The girl got a two-skip throw and was delighted.

I also made sure they were walking well clear of the coconut trees, worried they'd be conked on the head by one and die, which was something I'd never considered before; before I had to look after someone else. And somewhere along that walk—somewhere between the coconut trees and the tide—I felt it. A shift.

I think the shift was me becoming an adult. I was entirely responsible for someone. Two someones. For their curiosity, for their hydration, and for their sunblock. I had to carry the toddler on my back while making sure the girl was still in sight and still safe... and still happy!

And more than that: I was passing something on. Something I hadn't even realised I'd inherited: Words, stories, reflexes. I was the adult, and they were the children, and the line between us had become defined not by age but by what was being transferred.

By the time we reached the water park, I was sunburnt, sore, and sticky with whatever had been leaking from the toddler's juice box. The aunties clapped when they saw us. The grandma nodded approvingly. Someone gave me a wet towel and a coconut with a straw in it. I sat down and, for the first time in my life, felt the quiet satisfaction of having looked after someone. But that was only five miles! And I had many miles ahead of me. And I knew that, if I was lucky, one day I'd have to look after someone for a lot more than five miles. And this was one of the many things that crossed my mind later, after the heat had bled from the day, as I looked up at that sideways storm.

The beach was empty. Everyone else had retreated to the comfort of sand-blasting showers, air-conditioned rooms, or late-night card games. The sand was damp and cool. The wind had picked up. The storm was already growing, dark clouds stacking, much like the decks of cards and poker chips inside.

I strolled down the beach until the lights of the hotels were far behind me. The only glow came from distant fishing boats and the occasional flicker of phosphorescence in the sand. Crabs scurried at my approach—tiny, translucent, absurdly fast. One paused near my toes and stared at me, as if evaluating whether I was a predator or just a confused bipedal lighthouse.

The storm began to speak. Not in thunder, but in light. Sheet lightning, long tendrils crawling sideways across the clouds. No forked bolts. No crashes. Just light moving laterally, as if the sky were drawing a map in negative.

Then back to darkness. And *then* the thunder, half a minute delayed... or precisely on time.

I stood there for what felt like hours. Feet submerged. Eyes on the sky. Not thinking. Not narrating. Just existing.

That's when the thoughts started flooding in, uninvited, unstructured. The first one was, *this water has been places.* This was water that had existed since before the dinosaurs. Water that had once been swallowed by whales. Spat by volcanoes. Water that had churned in the Thames, and even in the streams of my childhood village. Water that had passed through the oesophagus of Einstein, of Boudicca, of the Buddha. Water that had once been tears. That had been blood. That had been rain on the rooftops of centuries, rooftops that had now crumbled. And now it was tickling my toes.

I looked down and saw my reflection in the water. Not clearly. Just the suggestion of a face. A ripple. I felt tiny, in the best possible way. Not insignificant. Not meaningless. Rather, I felt connected to meaning itself. All of it. The idea of being a single lick of paint upon a grand tapestry, and that it was OK that I wasn't the artist.

That night, I didn't look back at my schooldays, worrying that I could have done better. I didn't look ahead at my future, worrying about what career I should pursue. I thought about now. I thought about this place, right here. A dip in the sand on a beach on an island off the coast of China, surrounded by a galaxy with more stars than the beach had grains of sand—than all the beaches on Earth had grains of sand, for that matter. Although, I couldn't see them right now. The stars were obscured by the storm.

I wondered if anyone else was marvelling at the storm before me. I wondered what other storms were going on, and whether any of them were as peaceful as this one. Had anyone in the history of China, let alone humanity, felt this precise combination of feelings?

How lonely it is to realise that no one will ever fully understand what it's like to be you, and how you will never truly know what it's like to be anyone else. No one will ever be you again, and no one ever has been.

I don't know what experiences other people have gone through in China, not really. I don't know how others have truly felt about the country or what it has meant to them. I've categorised this book as *non-fiction*, but there's nothing about this book that is unbiased and objectively true, because nothing ever can be. But what I can tell you is I was *there*. I was there, and I was watching closely, listening carefully, and feeling it all.

I hear people criticise countries and their people. Countries they have never been within a thousand miles of. People they've never met or whose complicated lives they've never even taken the time to imagine, because they're too caught up in their *own* complicated lives. I hear people scream their opinions on things. Their opinions, which are, of course, not opinions, but gospel truths, because they're more moral than everyone else and because they've watched five Instagram reels by people who have been fed the same, homogenised, biased, tainted perspective on complex issues. We are all at least occasionally guilty of this. Me included.

In the context of *China*, I was always told things by people. We had a game like this at school... and ironically, it was called 'Chinese whispers.' But most of these things were false, and the things that were true turned out to be only partly true, grossly oversimplified. I can see the utility in that—if we didn't oversimplify and close our ears to hard truths, our understanding would be un-understandable, and that's scary. We can only have a worldview when we whittle the world down into something we can hold in our hands and in our heads.

You can read about China. You can watch documentaries. You can study the language, the history, the politics. But until you've walked five miles down a Chinese beach, carrying a sunburnt toddler on your shoulders with a leaking juice box, I maintain that you haven't experienced China.

That night, I walked back slowly. I did manage one blurry photo of the sideways storm, but I soon gave up. Some memories aren't for posting. Some are for *having*. You tuck them into the folds of your mind like a pressed flower in a notebook. You open them years later, and the scent is still there. Faint, but unmistakable. When you post it to Facebook, it becomes a post... not a memory.

Hainan was not the most exciting place I visited in China, but it gave me something I hadn't known I needed. Sometimes you think you know everything, or at least, you think you've sussed out how the world works. And then out of nowhere, there's a sideways Sanya storm, and it thunders down on you with a chaotic chorus of wisdom and perspective.

"My neck is sticky with juice and dribble,
And my ears are ringing from high-pitched screams and laughter.
But, still, I have a big smile on my face."

– Day 300

Canned Water

In China, people drink hot water. That's the norm. And I don't mean tea—just plain, steaming, hot water. At work, at school, on the train. You'll see people holding little vacuum flasks like it's a national sport. It's not just a quirk; it's a belief. Cold water is considered bad for you—it messes with your *qi,* your internal balance. Ask a Chinese friend why they drink hot water, and they'll look at you like you just asked whether gravity is optional. "Cold water is bad for your stomach," they'll say, as if it's written into the body's instruction manual. "It makes you fat."

So when I saw canned water for the first time, I was immediately intrigued. A gleaming aluminium can, almost always blue and silver as I remember, filled not with beer or Sprite but with flat, room-temperature water. It looked like something out of a prank show. But no, this was real—and not only real but common. You could get it in convenience stores next to juice boxes and packets of crisps—all of those rebelliously Western snacks.

If I'm not mistaken, this canned water was originally marketed towards children, or perhaps *teenagers,* more specifically. A kind of Western-style novelty. The irony, of course, is that we don't even have canned water in the West. (Well, we do have it, but it's not exactly common.) It was seen as a cool, foreign entity—something sleek and convenient. Refreshing. And I guess it was. But it was also exceedingly weird the first time I cracked open a can of still water, heard that gentle hiss, and then... tasted absolutely nothing. My brain was waiting for sugar, or fizz, or at least the mild disappointment of off-brand cola. But nope. Just water. From a can.

As I said, canned water exists in the West, but the whole idea seems very un-Western to me. Look, it's fine. There's nothing wrong with *canned* water. I mean, there's no major functional difference between it being canned as opposed to bottled. But... It's just really weird, alright?

My point is this: That experience, the mental whiplash of familiar packaging delivering something completely unexpected, is a pretty good metaphor for a lot of life in China. Things may look familiar, but they play by completely different rules. And those rules aren't worse. They're just... *theirs.*

Take public transport. As I mentioned in a previous chapter, the trains are fast, spotless, and always on time. But there's no concept of 'personal space.' People stand shoulder to shoulder, armpit to nostril, without a flicker of awkwardness. No one apologises for bumping into you, because everyone's bumping into everyone. It's not rude, it's just efficient. The goal is to get from point A to B.

Or dining out. You don't just get one dish and eat it yourself. You eat together, from shared plates, with chopsticks flying like swords mid-duel. People reach across you, serve you bits of chicken skin you didn't ask for, and encourage you to **chī duō yīdiǎn** (*eat a bit more*), even when you're full to bursting. You feel completely overwhelmed at first. Then one day, you're pouring soy sauce on someone else's dumplings like it's the most natural thing in the world. It's not worse. It's just different.

Back to the canned water. It became a kind of quiet symbol for me. A reminder that just because something isn't what you're used to, it doesn't mean it's wrong. I'd crack open a can before a train ride, or walking home through the sticky heat, and feel this sort of amused admiration. Someone thought this was a good idea—and you know what? It kind of is.

In the UK, and really in any country on Earth, we have this quiet assumption that our way is either normal or better. China knocked that out of me pretty quickly. If you're interested, here are some other minor differences that stuck out:

1) ***Boiled fruit juice:*** *Some people serve orange juice warm. Not hot, but well beyond room temperature.*
2) ***Sun umbrellas:*** *In China, pale skin is considered beautiful. Women walk around in the blazing sun holding delicate umbrellas. Whole streets look like they're caught in an invisible drizzle.*
3) ***No oven culture:*** *Most homes don't have ovens. Baking just isn't a thing unless you're at a Western-style café. And good Lord, you miss it—the smell of fresh bread or a proper roast.*
4) ***WeChat is everything:*** *It's like your WhatsApp, Facebook, Instagram, PayPal, and your diary rolled into one. You scan QR codes to pay, add friends, reserve restaurants, unlock bikes.*
5) ***Children wear split pants:*** *Like, literally pants with a slit down the middle so they can pee wherever. It's efficient, and kind of charming in its own way, until you see a toddler relieving themselves into a drain next to your foot, or you see a dad holding his kid over a public bin. Not nice.*

But still, most of these things—the canned water, the hot water, the boiled juice, the QR code payments—remind you, again and again, that you're 'not in Kansas anymore.' But they also remind you how arbitrary culture can be. The lines between 'normal' and 'weird' are just things we learned once and forgot were optional.

Canned water is flat, lukewarm, and a little confusing. But it's also kind of refreshing in a way that is not markedly different from bottled water. Like many other things, it's not trying to impress you. It just is what it is. And once you stop comparing everything to home, you start to appreciate the alternative, parallel-universe logic behind it.

"I was horrified today when I sipped a can of water
That just tasted like water. But I guess
It's okay to be surprised by normal."

– Day 21

The Window Ledge Bed

The Lee family had a maid, as did many wealthy families in China. She cooked most meals and cleaned up after them, washed clothes that weren't hers, swept floors that weren't hers, scrubbed toilets she didn't use, and politely averted her eyes whenever she walked in on a conversation that wasn't meant for her. And yet, strangely, she felt like part of the family. Not quite like a relative, not quite like a tenant—more like a long-standing piece of furniture with a cheerful attitude and great stamina.

She was in her early fifties, I think, with leathery skin from too many years in the sun. Her Mandarin was oddly soft around the edges due to a lack of schooling. She couldn't read or write at all. She smiled a lot. Not in the way people smile when they're told to, or when they want something, but in that natural way people do when they find things funny, or when they're trying to put you at ease. She was one of the friendliest people I met.

The Lees treated her well, in the way that kind employers treat someone who gives their heart to the company. She ate what they ate, laughed at their jokes, and got small gifts on birthdays. Once a month, she'd vanish for a weekend—off to visit family, I was told, though no one could tell me exactly where they lived or how far away they were. She'd return with a fresh pomegranate or some herbal sweets and quietly take up her station by the sink again.

The Lees were a decent family. They washed their own bowls, helped clear up when guests came, and were eternally grateful for what they had. They took nothing for granted. Even the children treated the maid with utmost respect. In the small ecosystem of privilege, they weren't tyrants. But they still had an in-house maid. And more important, at least to me, was where the maid slept.

On a window ledge.

Yes. A window ledge. Not a metaphor. Not a brand of minimalist futon. A literal, lacquered-wood-plank ledge, about two feet deep and barely six long, cushioned with a folded quilt and a foam mat as thin as a burger van menu.

What's worse, the ledge bed was in the parents' bedroom, set into the far wall like an architectural afterthought, and technically large enough to accommodate a sleeping human being in the way a suitcase technically fits into an overhead locker. I didn't see it straight away. But once I did, I couldn't unsee it.

She'd curl up there at night with the quilt tucked under her chin and her back to the glass, like a cat seeking warmth. There was no curtain, no partition, no sense of privacy—just her and the murmured bedtime routines of her employers a few feet away. I once asked her whether it was uncomfortable. She said no. She smiled again.

And maybe it wasn't. Maybe, to her, that small ledge in the Lees' quiet, modern apartment was already worlds better than wherever she'd come from. Maybe she had her own room back home, or maybe she didn't. Maybe she saw that window ledge not as humiliation, but as security. A soft place to sleep. A job that came with meals, and respect, and something resembling company.

But still. *A window ledge?*

In China, where family is everything and four generations often live under one roof, privacy is a flexible concept. It's not unusual for grandparents to sleep in the same room as the couple, or for children and parents to share a space that, in the West, would be considered absurdly cramped. When I first saw this, I thought, *how on Earth do you get any sleep?* Yet this closeness is about more than just economics—it's about duty, respect, and the invisible threads that keep families together.

Still, watching the maid sleep on a ledge in the parents' room was a different matter. It screamed of a social distance that no cultural practice could soften. The maid's presence was a constant, a hum running through the household. She was always there, always doing something: chopping vegetables, washing clothes, tidying toys. Yet, she was invisible in many ways. Not deliberately—no one was cruel. It was the silent social order, the unspoken understanding of who belonged and who served.

Her lack of literacy and formal education set her apart more than anything else. In China, education is the most powerful currency. The difference between the Lees and their maid was not just about money; it was about knowledge, language, and opportunity. While the Lees spoke fluent Mandarin with confident tones, used smartphones and apps effortlessly, and debated university or school choices, the maid's speech was simple, her vocabulary limited. She didn't read books, newspapers, or websites. She couldn't text in Chinese characters. The world she inhabited was smaller, defined more by routine and repetition than by curiosity or ambition.

This divide is not unique to this family or even to China. Yet, seeing it so closely, day after day, made the gulf feel very real.

At the same time, I wondered—who was I to judge her life? Happiness is not always about education or material comfort. Perhaps she found contentment in small things: a shared laugh, a meal well cooked, a quiet moment in the sun. Perhaps her life had its own dignity, its own rhythms I would never fully understand. And in that sense, she could have been the wealthiest member of the household.

But regardless, as far as I could comprehend, the bed itself was both a symbol and a reality. It symbolised the inequalities baked into Chinese society—the rapid economic growth leaving some behind as others flourished. It was a reminder that behind gleaming skyscrapers and luxury apartments, there were millions barely scraping by.

Yet, the reality of that ledge was also simple. It was a bed. A place to rest after a long day's work. It was not a cage or a punishment. It was, in its own way, a home. There is something haunting about the idea of someone sleeping in such a narrow space, day after day, surrounded by comfort they do not share but which sustains them.

Perhaps the most difficult question is this: Who decides what is enough? In the West, we often measure poverty or hardship by standards of space, privacy, and possessions. But in other cultures, the calculus of satisfaction is different.

The maid never complained. She smiled. She worked hard. She seemed content. And for all I know, she might have felt lucky to have that ledge, that job, and the family who gave her both. So, as much as the window ledge bed struck me as unfair, as stark, as painfully unequal, I was also forced to confront my own assumptions. Was I imposing my values on her life? Was her discomfort really, in some way, *mine?*

Though the country as a whole has experienced exponential economic growth, the window ledge bed is still, quite literally, a window into China's vast class disparities—between urban and rural, rich and poor, educated and uneducated. In this way, it is a stark reminder that China's story is not just about gleaming progress and booming cities. It is also about the people who live quietly in the shadows of that progress.

"I struggled to sleep last night.
Why do I get my own bed?
Do I deserve one?"

– Day 15

Chongqinghua

When I first started learning Mandarin at the Chongqing Technology and Business University (CTBU), I was pumped. Textbooks, audio drills, pinyin charts—I soaked it all up like a sponge. The only problem? What I learned in the classroom was Beijing Mandarin, also known as Putonghua—the official standard dialect of China. The only problem is that Chinese has about a hundred dialects, and even in the municipality of Chongqing (which, in theory, should bring heavy influence from the capital), they have their own way of speaking. Chongqinghua. A vibrant local dialect that is as spicy and bold as the city itself. It was like learning English and landing in Glasgow—same language, but entirely different rhythms, sounds, and expressions. If you weren't prepared, you might as well have been listening to an alien transmission.

But what is Mandarin, anyway?

First, let's untangle some basics. Mandarin is the main official language of China. Putonghua is a standardised form based mostly on the Beijing dialect. It's the version taught in schools, used in government, and heard on state media. Think of RP in the UK, only much more alive and widely spoken. China is a vast country, and its people speak a dizzying variety of dialects and languages. Cantonese in Guangdong, Shanghainese in Shanghai, Hokkien in Fujian, and so on.

Mandarin itself isn't uniform. The Putonghua you learn in a classroom is a simplified, polished version. The reality on the street is messier. Regional accents, slang, tonal shifts, and entirely different vocabulary often confuse learners.

Enter Chongqinghua.

Chongqinghua is a Southwestern Mandarin dialect, but it has unique sounds and expressions that set it apart from Beijing's Putonghua. I like to think of the city's dialect as loud, fast, and spicy, mirroring Chongqing's fiery hot pot and humid summer air.

One of the most noticeable features of Chongqinghua is the substitution of the "*ts*" sound for the standard "*ch.*" For example, the Putonghua word "chī" (*to eat*) might sound like "tsī" in Chongqinghua. It's subtle but distinctive, a linguistic spice that tickles your ears and screams, "This is Chongqing, baby."

The intonation is also different—a bit rougher, with a faster rhythm, as if the words themselves are steaming hot and need to be said quickly before they cool off.

Chongqing is a relatively new mega-city in terms of urban scale. In the last few decades, it has transformed from a collection of small towns and river ports into one of China's largest metropolises, a sprawling urban jungle with over thirty million residents. This explosive growth brought people from various parts of Sichuan and beyond, all blending their own speech patterns into the local dialect.

Chongqinghua reflects this fusion: It's dynamic, evolving, and resistant to the smooth, official Putonghua spoken in Beijing. It's a badge of identity for locals, a way of saying, "I'm

Chinese, but I'm *also* Chongqing-ese." In a way, it's quite rebellious.

I started my time in Chongqing feeling a bit lost. The Mandarin I learned was barely enough to make a dent in conversations. People spoke fast, dropped syllables, and peppered their speech with local slang I hadn't previously encountered. But slowly, I took it on as a challenge. I mimicked the strange sounds, picked up the local phrases, and tried to match their quick cadence. I practiced with neighbours, vendors, and my host family. There were many moments of confusion, frustration, and yes, embarrassment.

Yet, eventually, something magical happened. I found myself actually *speaking* Chongqinghua. Locals smiled wider when I used their dialect. It was a bridge into their lives and culture. Some of my Mandarin-speaking friends from other provinces found my speech confusing—a humorous reminder that even *within* China, language can be a puzzle box. Even now, back in the UK, I find myself slipping into Chongqinghua expressions and pronunciation when I do speak Mandarin. (Although, regrettably, I don't spend much time speaking Chinese these days.) It's my linguistic souvenir—part of my identity and connection to that wild, vibrant city.

Dialects, in China, are more than just ways of speaking. They carry deep cultural, historical, and social significance. Speaking Chongqinghua ties you to the city's history of rivers and mountains, spicy food, and unyielding spirit. It signals where you come from, your social circle, and your attitude, and I think that is especially important under a government so obsessed with national unity and assimilation.

For locals, hearing someone speak in their dialect, even imperfectly, is a sign of respect and belonging. It's a way of softening the outsider's edge. For foreigners, adopting a local dialect can open doors, but it also shows just how complex language is in China—a nation whose voices are plural, not singular.

Here are a few phrases to give you a taste of Chongqinghua:

- ***Lo***— *A common particle added at the end of sentences, giving a sense of finality or emphasis. For example,* **hǎo lo** *means "Alright then!" or "That's settled!"*
- ***Pa***— *Used more loosely than in standard Mandarin, often meaning "Worry."*
- ***Záo***— *Short for "good morning," but said casually with a rising tone* ***záo*** *instead of* ***zǎo*** .

With modernisation and internal migration, Putonghua's dominance grows. Schools push it; TV and media favour it. Some fear dialects like Chongqinghua might fade or be 'standardised out.' But language, like culture, resists simple erasure. In China, dialects still thrive in homes, markets, and streets. They are woven into daily life, from casual greetings to laughter and jokes. They carry history, belonging, and identity.

Chongqinghua is more than a dialect. It's the city's voice—spicy, bold, and fast. It's the sound of hot pot bubbling, rivers rushing, and the laughter of millions. For me, learning it was a way to truly *live* in Chongqing, rather than simply *stay* there.

"If you want to make someone smile, learn their language.
If you want to make them cry, learn their dialect."

– Day 298

Hot Pot Sweat

You can't talk about China, particularly Southwestern China, without talking about hot pot. And in the region where I lived, you didn't *eat* hot pot. You survived it. You didn't sit at the table, waiting for it to arrive. *It* waited for *you* to arrive. It was ready long before you were, a liquid volcano—angry, bubbling, and red. Ready to erupt. A broth so saturated with dried chillies and Sichuan peppercorns it looked less like soup and more like the burning mantle of Hell. In the centre of the table, it hissed and spat like it wanted a fight. Floating in it were bright red oil slicks, entire garlic cloves, medicinal roots, ancient bark, and so many chillies it looked like a bouquet arranged by someone with a personal vendetta.

And next to it, mostly untouched, as if only there to appease the foreigners, a pale yin to the angry red yang—a quiet, flavourless broth, benign, and milky, and a bit embarrassed to even be there. That's the white soup. You dip things into it when you're not feeling brave. When you need a break. When your stomach lining begins to mutter a suicidal soliloquy.

You've never broken a sweat until you've had hot pot. Summers, especially Chongqing summers, are already notorious. The city is built in a basin, hemmed in by hills and wet with humidity. It feels like walking through an open mouth. And then someone says, "Shall we go for hot pot?"

Of course you go. You go because everyone else goes, and because it's what friends do, and because you don't want to be the foreigner who says 'no' to a new experience. Right? You go because deep down, you know you'll enjoy it. Or you'll at least endure it together.

The establishments themselves are cavernous—great echoing spaces with colossal tables, and neon signs, and fans that have long since given up trying. Most are open-air or at least pretend to be, offering the illusion of ventilation. The table is usually circular, and in the middle, sunken into the surface like a ritualistic pit, is the fire. Surrounding that fire is everyone—twenty people crammed around a rotating tabletop, laughing, shouting, sweating through their T-shirts as meat sizzles and lungs sting. You wipe your face with tissues that dissolve in your hand. You reach for your drink, and your fingers slide off the condensation. It's chaos. Beautiful, spicy chaos.

The process is as important as the food. First, you order a selection of things you want to endanger your life with. Thinly sliced meat, lotus root, potatoes, wood ear mushrooms, tofu skin, quail eggs, bamboo shoots. You can get intestines if you're brave, or brain if you're insane.

Next comes the sauce. You walk to the sauce station like it's a sacred pilgrimage. It's a bar of opportunity—finely chopped garlic, fermented tofu, coriander, crushed peanuts, soy, vinegar, chilli oil. But the real secret, as everyone will tell you, is the sesame oil. You take a small white bowl and pour it in, about halfway. This is your shield. Your only line of defence. You dip the fiery meat into the oil before it enters your mouth. It doesn't put out the fire, but it adds flavour and creates the illusion of safety, like wearing a bicycle helmet on a raging bull.

The first bite is always shocking. A little square of duck, fished from the red pit, steam still rising. You dunk it in oil. You take a breath. You bite. And then—it hits. A numbing, tingling wave of heat. The Sichuan peppercorn doesn't burn like chilli. It buzzes. It makes your lips go electric and your tongue forget its job. It's not so much pain as it is confusion. Your face begins to leak. You make strange sounds. Someone passes you a beer or baijiu. Someone else laughs because it's your first time.

But somewhere, halfway through the meal, something changes. The pyromaniacal pain becomes normal. You stop resisting. Your sinuses clear. Your head lightens. You begin to talk. Really talk.

Hot pot, I learned, is not just food. It's a form of group therapy.

You start with small talk—weather, TV shows, the tragic state of your mouth. But as the sweat drips down your back and your arms stick to the table, you relax. You say things you didn't plan to say. You share stories you usually keep folded up. You ask questions you'd normally be too polite to voice. It's as though the hot broth simmers away your social restraint. The sweat opens up your pores, and at the same time, your entire soul.

Once, at a hot pot dinner, I asked my host father about his job. He had never spoken about it before, at least, not in any detail. But with red soup bubbling and his collar soaked through, he told me about the immense stress he was under at work. I won't tell you what he did, but I can tell you it was something important to the lives of ordinary people, and in a subliminal way, to the growth and continued success of the nation. At any other time of day, or night, rain or shine, whether he was completely sober or utterly tanked, my host father was reticent on matters of work. But something about hot pot opened him up—as it did any other person—to the possibility of garrulity, frankness, and even outspokenness. On these rare occasions, the tirelessly optimistic and content Mr Lee would talk of his anxieties and regrets. But he would also talk about his dreams, small and big—and though his bigger dreams might be enough to fill a whole book, I'd like to share one of his lesser dreams with you in the next chapter.

Once you survive your first hot pot, you crave the next one. You want to try weirder vegetables. You want to go spicier. You start learning words like **wēilà** (*mild spicy*) and **zhōnglà** (*medium spicy*), and you argue about which dipping sauce is superior. You seek out the sketchiest, smokiest hot pot joints because they always have the best broth. You start texting people: "Hot pot tonight?" But it's not really for the devilish food. It's for the experience. It's for the next hot pot conversation. It's for the feeling of togetherness, of shared pain and pleasure, of communal combustion. There's something beautiful about watching a group of people sit shoulder to shoulder, united by nothing more than oil, fire, and bravery.

And then there's the silence at the end. The broth grows weary. The flames dim. People lean back, sighing, flushed and limp, holding their bellies and mumbling about how they'll never eat again. The napkins on the table are no longer white, far from it. The floor is slick with dropped chopsticks and runaway mushrooms. The air is thick with chilli and triumph. You leave the restaurant dizzy, drunk on capsaicin and conversation. Your clothes smell like a laundry basket. Your stomach hums. Somehow, you feel closer to the people you came in with, as though you have survived something together.

For flavour, not so much, but for garrulity, candour, and communal triumph, I admire hot pot.

"There's an important word that I need to jot down.
It's up there with 'help' and 'water.'
***Là**—the Chinese word for spice."*

– Day 18

One of Shushu's Lesser Dreams

To my Chinese host family, I wasn't a guest. I really *was* a member of the family. Or at least, they made me feel that way. They called me **érzi** (meaning *son*), and they insisted I call them **āyí** (*aunty*), and **shūshu** (*uncle*). I called the children **dìdi** (*little brother*)—OK, so I know that doesn't technically add up, but that's just how it is in China. I guess you had to be there. And so in this chapter, as requested six years ago, I'm going to refer to Mr Lee as 'Shushu.'

Shushu was successful by any metric. He was wealthy, hard-working, and wise. He had a loving wife, proud parents, and two healthy children. Plus, as I mentioned in the previous chapter, his job was important. His job required innovation, tenacity, and a seemingly endless continuum of late nights. It was normal for Shushu to come home at ten or even eleven o'clock, at which point he would pour himself soup or tea and go down into the basement.

Down there, you would find a biome of parchment, scrolls, notebooks, and blueprints. Though curiously, he only had one pencil. There were floor plans for future homes, business ideas, and financial Plan Bs. Mega-projects unfurled on every wall. When I think of Shushu, I think of pupil-shrinking glasses, tea, and ambition. But amongst the mammothian dreams, he had a lesser one—a simpler one. And one rainy Saturday morning, he showed it to me.

The children's English was good, the mother's was elementary, and the father's was non-existent. He spoke to me exclusively in Chinese. Not only that, but he spoke fast and quietly, and so most of the time I had no idea what was going on.

Shushu: "Have you had breakfast, son?"

Me: "Yes, thank you."

Shushu: "Are you busy today?"

Me: "I'm looking after the youngest brother today."

Shushu: "Ah, you're not. He is at his aunt's. So does that mean you're free to help me?"

Me: "Of course. What do you need help with?"

Shushu: "I will show you. Come, come."

I can still hear that word so crisply—**Lái** (*come on*). The word is magnetic. It beckons, it goes straight to your feet, well before it reaches your ears.

We went down to floor -2, into the large garage shared by the whole neighbourhood. From there, we took the family car out into the city. Because of the mist and because of the city's sprawl, it was hard to tell when you were reaching the end of it, but I knew we were going somewhere new. Somewhere I had never been before. Not the airport to hop on a domestic flight, not to the city centre, but *out*. For the first couple of hours, it was just more city, unrelentingly. But after a certain mile-long bridge, the city finally stopped, giving way to a new kind of megalopolis... the jungle. I don't know if 'jungle' is the geographically correct term, but it will do the best job at painting an accurate picture. A thousand shades of green. Oppressive humidity. Watchful monkeys.

I could see that whatever I was about to help with was important, maybe even dangerous. There was a blueprint on the dashboard with a detailed plan in white ink and a wild assortment of notes dotted around the edge. I could feel the car was slightly tilted on its rear wheels, and so I knew we were carrying something heavy in the boot.

We journeyed all day, deep into the next province. Only when the sun had set on the jungle, nestled between two magnolia-covered mountains, did we arrive at our destination. By then, I couldn't see anything. I was so used to the bright city lights that the meagre lanterns were of little use to me.

Shushu (turning the key in the ignition): "We have arrived."

Silence. We got out of the car. Mosquitoes. Lots of mosquitoes.

Me: "Where are we?"

He told me, but I didn't understand his answer.

Shushu: "OK, you will sleep now. Here, this building. Go upstairs and find a bed. Come back here in the morning. Six o'clock."

He said this eagerly, pointing at the ground in front of him.

The bedroom upstairs was literally that—a bedroom. It was a room, and there was a bed, and nothing else. OK, that's not true. There were also blinds. In any case, I slept until the early morning, by which time the orange sun squinted through the shutter blinds from way over the mountains.

Now everything had been rendered: The barn and the two houses, the ploughs, the sloping fields, the goats (who were well-adapted to said sloping fields), and the acres of wild forests and steep hills that surrounded us. Shushu was talking to an old couple who were wearing straw hats—his parents. I understood then. This was *their* home, a home where he hoped, one day, to retire.

It turned out the blueprints on the dashboard were for a garden, and the great weight in the boot was comprised of exotic plants and stones, the likes of which he could only find in the city. Thus, the morning was spent digging, planting, watering, and shifting wheelbarrows of soil.

When we were done, he took up a machete and handed me an axe. Were we about to duel? No. We needed them to get through the thick, unruly forest. "**Lái**," he kept saying. We ventured deeper and deeper into the vegetation, chopping through leaves, vines, and grass blades. My axe came in handy for half-fallen branches and obtrusive stumps. Then there was a steep incline. It was exhausting. Climb, chop, climb, chop, through humid, forty-degree heat. I thought to myself: *This better be worth it.*

Eventually, we made it to the top of a pointy hill, where we found a sort of clearing. Every now and then, in life—if you're paying attention—you will be presented with these awe-and-wonder moments. And on rare occasions, these awe-and-wonder moments make you cry. It's happened to me only a handful of times. This was one of those times.

I took a picture to show my family and friends back home, but then I soon deleted it. I deleted it because the photo didn't come anywhere *close* to giving the scene any form of justice. It was just perfect. And for the same reason, I'm not going to attempt to describe it now, other than to say this: It was a view. One of the most beautiful views I had ever seen. Hills folding into hills, folding into heavens, and heavens backstroking across layers of viridescent mist. And not a human in sight, other than me and Shushu. Will that do it? Not really.

He pointed towards the indeterminate horizon and said, "Beautiful." This word he actually said in English. Actually, he said "*bey-ta-fo,*" but that was close enough. Then he smiled. Then he pointed again, this time over my shoulder. Down at the bottom of the hill, you could just about make out the two houses and the barn, with a small splash of colour in front of them—the garden, now complete with flowers and stones. He then said something in Chinese which I did not understand. He could tell I was confused, so he said it louder, but that didn't help. He then proceeded to take out his phone to locate a note he had made. It appeared to be a list of English words that he had gathered from overhearing the lessons I gave his children. He found the word he was looking for and closed his phone. He pointed back at the garden.

Shushu: "Small... dree..."

Me: "Small *dream*?"

Shushu: "Small *dream*."

Then a brief pause.

Then, in Chinese, he said: "Come. I must return to the city. I must work."

Shushu's garden didn't become a regular feature of my time in China, but I *did* go back once or twice. It changed a little each time. Some of the plants had survived. Others hadn't. The rocks had shifted, or maybe they'd just looked different in my memory. But it was still there. Quiet. Oddly untouched. Like a sentence he'd started and never quite finished.

I don't think the garden was ever meant to be a commitment. It wasn't a retirement plan, or a pivot, or a statement. It was more like a gesture. A reminder that he could build something beautiful and unimportant, if he wanted to. That for one humid day, he could dig, and arrange, and plant—not for money, or prestige, or reputation, but just to see what might grow.

This patch of earth in the middle of the jungle was his escape. It felt almost rebellious to me. It wasn't scalable. It wasn't monetisable. It didn't have a KPI. It was just... a garden. And maybe that's why I remember it. Because in all the vivid, noisy, overstimulating moments of China, this one was unusually quiet. Shushu in his straw hat. Me digging half-heartedly in a patch of soil that didn't need me. No baijiu. No plans. Just some heat and some hope.

I realise that, in a way, this whole book is a garden too. A loose collection of strange, lived-in memories, grown in the cracks of a much bigger story. A plastic stool. A rail line through a building. A maid's bed. A bowl of soup so spicy it rearranged my insides. None of it fits into a brochure. But all of it started something—*planted* something—in me.

The garden, one of Shushu's lesser dreams, seemed trivial, pointless, and negligible next to the grand expanse of the neighbouring forests and mountain ranges, but for what it represented—a pause, a maybe, a what-if—I think I understood its significance.

"I've boiled it down to this:
The pursuit of something quiet and unnecessary
In a life that rarely allows for either."

– Day 136

Tree Root Tea

There's a kind of table in China that looks less like furniture and more like something you'd find in a fantasy novel—half sculpture, half shrine. It's carved from the roots of a tree, a heavy tangle of gnarled limbs and polished bulges, with flat surfaces just big enough to rest cups, with channels running through it for water drainage. Unlike most other things in China, these tables are not mass-produced. They're chosen. Carved from whole roots, smoothed by hand, and carried into teahouses and homes by two or three men with strong backs and a lot of patience.

The tea flows, not in pots, but in rounds. Cups that seem not much larger than thimbles are filled, emptied, filled again. And how do you ask for more? Not with words. The knock of fingertips on the table is the accepted terminology.

I am British, and so I know my way around a kettle. Before I lived in China, I drank tea like the British do: brewed from a bag, with milk, sugar, and perhaps the soggy ghost of a biscuit. It wasn't a ritual. It wasn't a culture, and if it was, it was a primitive one in comparison. I thought *tea* was just a means of warming up.

That changed somewhere between the third and fourth refill of **chá** (*tea*) at a roadside tea shop where the owner, an older woman with forearms like tree trunks, taught me the exact temperature I needed to boil water for different leaves. She poured, explained, poured again. When I reached for the cup, she slapped my hand and pointed to a tiny thermometer floating in her kettle. She'd shake her head.

"Not yet."

There's a reason tea in China doesn't taste rushed.

China's tea culture is deep enough to drown in, but I'll try to skim the surface here. First, the language. In Chinese, tea is classified mostly by colour—not in the literal sense, but in a poetic one. Each category has a history, a region, and a preparation method that's passed down more carefully than family heirlooms.

- ***Lǜ chá*** *(green tea): Light, grassy, sometimes floral. Needs lower temperatures (around 80°C) or it turns bitter.*
- ***Hóng chá*** *(red tea): What the West usually calls "black tea." Stronger, richer, oxidised. Brewed hotter.*
- ***Hēi chá*** *(black tea): Often aged, fermented, earthy. Think pu'er, which comes in bricks and tastes like damp forest floor in the best possible way.*
- ***Bái chá*** *(white tea): Delicate, lightly processed. Often from younger buds.*
- ***Huáng chá*** *(yellow tea): Rare, subtle, expensive. Somewhere between green and white.*

Each type demands a different technique—different kettles, different pots, even different moods. If you're angry, or upset, or in a rush, some tea masters will tell you not to brew anything at all. The leaves can tell. They'll punish you for your impatience.

In many homes, tea isn't just something you drink. It's something you *do*. Not just a noun but a verb. You prepare it, perform it, share it, and talk around it. The process usually begins with the kettle. Not the electric kind with a flip-top lid and a plastic base. A proper kettle is made of iron or copper, and it rests on a flame or induction heater. You don't just 'boil' water. You *bring it to the right moment*. For green tea, that's when the tiny fish-eye bubbles begin to form—*not* a full rolling boil.

Then comes the warming of the tea ware. The cups, the teapot (often a yixing clay one), and the filter are rinsed with hot water to prepare them for the leaves. You don't want to shock the tea. You want to welcome it, coax it open.

The first brew is often a rinse. Poured in, swirled, poured out. Then comes the real infusion—ten or twenty seconds at first, depending on the type. Then it's poured through a strainer into a pale cup called a **gōng dào bēi**, so that every guest gets the same strength.

The teacups are so small that by the time you've finished one, you want another. That's the idea. It keeps the conversation moving. It lets you drink slowly and together. In China, with food, tea, and many other things, no single person may hoard. Rather, the food (or tea) is stored in the centre, for everyone to share, in modest but frequent amounts.

As a history lover, I can't help but be reminded of Mao Zedong's communist collectivisation campaign during the 'Great Leap Forward' of the 1950s. Many people speculate that communism gave way to many of the modern Chinese mentalities, but sitting at the tree root, interacting with the ancient practice of tea-making, I couldn't help but wonder if it was the mentality that gave way to the form of government. Of course, the truth is much more complicated than that, I know. In any event, it is inaccurate to call modern-day China *solely* communist, seeing as it has embraced many aspects of capitalism. China is complex and unfathomable.

Let's go back to that tree root table for a moment. It's not just aesthetic. It's functional. The indentations, channels, and holes in the surface are designed to catch overflow, because with proper Chinese tea-making, *you spill a lot*. It's the only time when spilling isn't an accident. You're rinsing cups, over-pouring, and emptying the pot before it stews. Water is always flowing.

The tea master will often have a drainage bucket hidden beneath the table, connected to the built-in grooves and spouts. They wipe the cups with a cloth, flick the waste tea aside, and begin again. It's simultaneously messy and elegant. And there's something deeply grounding about it all. The root, once buried underground, now anchors the space for human connection. You sit low. You hunch. You lean forward. It's intimate. Unlike coffee, which often signals productivity or speed, tea in China signals stillness. You don't gulp it on the go. You sit. You stay. Coffee means *what will be*. Tea means *what is*. Tea means *now*.

There's a kind of presence and openness, an unrushed honesty that floats to the surface with tea. Maybe it's the repetition, the rhythm. Pour, sip, talk. Pour, sip, listen. But often, there is just silence. The most comfortable silence imaginable, a silence that is broken only by the clink of lids, the whistle of water, and the occasional knock on wood.

There's no official 'end' to a tea session. Sometimes the leaves give out. Sometimes the sun gives out first. Usually, there's a lull in the conversation, and someone begins tidying up, slowly. The kettle is emptied, the table wiped. Cups stacked. Nobody rushes off. There's no alarm. Just a nod, a satisfied sigh, maybe a joke. You leave with your chest warmer and your mind clearer. You've done nothing, really, but it feels like a lot. That's the magic of tree root tea.

"Today I worked out that a different culture
Is just a rearrangement of priorities.
What my hosts spend on cars, they spend
Double on clothing. What they spend on clothing,
They spend triple on tea. For most people in the West,
It's the reverse order."

– Day 192

Face Jobs and Face Masks

It was always the subway where it hit me hardest. The Sky Rail. Chongqing's iconic, levitating rollercoaster of a public transport system offered the kind of vantage you don't get in most cities. Suspended above highways, and rivers, and balconies strung with washing, it rushed you past lives in progress, but it also turned you inward. With the windows on either side flashing and flickering like old film reels, you were left to look at your fellow passengers. And they, mostly, were looking at their phones.

But if you did look up, and if you did pay attention, you started to notice something. The faces. I'm talking about the faces of young women. Always so smooth. So sculpted. So luminous. It became almost a game in my head, one I played in silence, half curious, half uncomfortable. Real or not? Natural or modified? Skin-whitened or just illuminated by good lighting?

Plastic surgery, face masks, whitening creams, filters—the full artillery of beauty modification is alive and well in China, and especially visible in urban hubs like Chongqing. This wasn't something I went hunting for, mind you. It was there, as present as hot pot steam.

Let's start with the big one: Eye surgery. Double eyelid surgery, or **shuāng yǎnpí zhěngróng**, is practically a rite of passage for some circles of young women, especially those living in the city. The surgery creates a visible fold in the eyelid, which is considered to make the eye appear bigger and more 'alert.' This feature, seen as a marker of beauty, also happens to be more commonly found in Western or mixed-heritage individuals. And while that raises a whole box of complicated questions about cultural standards and internalised ideals, it also felt—to someone on the outside, like me—strangely ubiquitous.

I met a girl once at a language exchange who casually mentioned her eye surgery as if it were no more consequential than changing her hairstyle. "It makes my job interviews easier," she said. "People trust faces that look awake." Not prettier—just more employable. It wasn't about seduction; it was about survival. As I recall, that girl was actually Thai, but a Thai person working in China nonetheless.

And then there's the skin. The ideal skin tone in many parts of China is **báixī**—pale, fair, unblemished. 'Snow white' as a compliment doesn't feel like a fairy tale here; it's a literal goal. You can walk into a supermarket and find ten rows of whitening products, each with a smiling model who looks like she's been lit up from within by a fluorescent bulb.

These creams promise not just fairness, but success. Fairness is still too often linked to status, to indoor office jobs, and air-conditioned cars. I once asked a colleague why she avoided the sun with such militancy. "I worked hard to get out of the countryside," she said. "I'm not going to go backwards."

And this was not some fringe phenomenon. It was visible everywhere. On buses. In cafes. And especially, as I said, on the metro. Face masks—long before the pandemic made them global—were already a staple of beauty and privacy. Not surgical masks, though they appeared too. I'm talking about fashion masks. Soft, pastel, often embroidered with cartoon characters or slogans like *Don't Talk to Me* or *Princess on Duty*. They served a dual purpose: protection from pollution and camouflage for makeup-less days or healing from surgeries.

The pressure, though, felt immense. For women in particular, appearance seemed to be not just a personal choice but a social obligation. Your face was your business card, your resume, your public broadcast channel. There was this unspoken expectation that a young woman in the city would "know how to look after herself," which—translated—often meant "know how to alter herself."

Yet, all this said, I never once found these women vain. Not once. That's not me being diplomatic; it's the honest truth. There was a kind of quiet resilience to it. They were doing what they had to do in a world where, often, image was currency. They weren't shallow; they were strategists.

Beauty talk came up often at university. Students would point to idols on their phones and dissect their faces like critics at a sculpture unveiling. "His jaw is ninety degrees," one girl said dreamily about a pop star. "Like a ruler."

Another said, "Her skin is so white it glows."

And yet, for all that—all the surgery, the creams, the filters, the quiet battles fought in front of bathroom mirrors—it would be a mistake to paint Chinese beauty culture as dystopian. It's intense, sure. But it's also... creative. Fluid. It allows for play. There's a kind of artfulness to it that I came to admire. The way someone could transform their look with tiny changes. The way expression wasn't fixed but was evolving.

At first, it looked like autonomy and independence. It looked like individuality. But is it individualistic to *choose* to follow strict fashion trends... or is it the opposite?

One of my favourite things was watching older women at the dancing squares in the evening. They sported bright lipstick, floral scarves, and contradictory colours. They wore creases, lines, and wrinkles proudly.

Meanwhile, the younger generations were swimming through a sea of conflicting expectations. Be pretty, but not fake. Be pale, but not sickly. Be modern, but not unorthodox. Be effortless, but put-together. And in the middle of it all: the face. The face as symbol. As tool. As battlefield.

There's no moral high ground here. Just differences. Just histories. Just societies built on different assumptions. In any case, many things about this dynamic are reflected in the West, as I am constantly reminded by young women in particular. I am aware of this. I am sensitive to it, and am left wondering what I can do to fight it. But there are differences between the way this phenomenon presents in China and the West. The very fact that we are even having a conversation about it might be the first one.

I do think often of that subway game—*Real or Not*. And I think now, maybe I had it wrong. Maybe the better question isn't, *is it fake?* But rather, *why does it matter?* Because behind every sculpted eyelid or powdered cheek is a person trying to find their place in this world. To be seen in the way they want. And I think, deep down, that's universal.

"In this metro carriage, there are at least two hundred faces.
And yet, there are only fifty people.
Or is it the other way around?"

– Day 245

Chopsticks

(You knew this was coming.)

When I first arrived in China, the humble chopstick—or **kuàizi** as it's called—was a source of endless frustration, embarrassment, and determination.

I had grown up with forks, knives, spoons, and even fingers when it came to certain foods. But these two slender sticks, poised so effortlessly between the thumb and fingers of every Chinese person I met, were like some sort of magic wand. They seemed so simple. So elegant. So deceptively easy. For me, they were the ultimate test of dexterity and patience.

At first, my attempts to pick up noodles looked more like a slapstick comedy routine than a graceful meal. Dumplings were squashed. Steamed rice was somehow de-steamed. And those little slippery pieces of tofu? They laughed in the face of my fumbling fingers. The more I tried, the more people watched. I could sense the silent judgment. (Although now that I think about it, the judgement wasn't silent at all.)

Meals became a battleground. Every breakfast, lunch, and dinner became a challenge to conquer this simple tool. These two pieces of wood.

I remember one particularly humiliating evening at a crowded hot pot restaurant where, in the middle of a boil-and-dip frenzy, I managed to lose control and launch a slippery mushroom halfway across the table. The whole room fell silent for a split second, then burst out laughing. I left alone, red-faced, plotting my revenge against the kuaizi.

But slowly, things began to change.

A local friend gave me some tips: Relax your hand, don't squeeze too hard, think of the chopsticks as a pair of scissor blades. I watched already-dexterous children at the next table, practiced copying their nimble fingers, and began to understand the rhythm and flow. Before long, I was picking up noodles without breaking them, grabbing dumplings with ease, and even managing the dreaded slippery tofu cubes.

Now, years later, I wield my chopsticks like a pro. In fact, whenever I go to a Chinese restaurant in the UK with my fellow countrymen, it's a source of mild annoyance and endless teasing. There I am, expertly lifting morsels with the flick of a wrist, while they stare, wrists awry, grumbling about how "These things are useless" or asking, "Why don't they just use a knife and fork?"

I realise I'm sounding awfully smug and quasi-cultured. But when you've been laughed at by a room full of Chinese people, you *have* to be smug about it.

Chopsticks are more than just utensils. They are a lens into Chinese history, culture, and psychology. Historically, chopsticks date back over three thousand years, showing up at some point during the Shang Dynasty. They were initially utilitarian tools for cooking and serving food, especially when dealing with the intense heat of fire and pots.

Over centuries, they evolved into the everyday eating implements we know today, perfectly suited to a cuisine that consists of bite-sized pieces, communal dining, and an emphasis on balance and harmony.

Sociologically, chopsticks reflect Chinese values of community and sharing. Meals in China are rarely about individual plates and private portions. Instead, dishes are placed in the centre, shared by all at the table. The chopsticks are the connectors, delicate extensions of the hand that reach out to these communal dishes, bringing food to one's bowl.

Culturally, chopsticks speak to Chinese ideas of precision, balance, and respect. The very design—two identical sticks that must be perfectly coordinated—embodies harmony and cooperation. Learning to use chopsticks is like learning a dance. It requires concentration and patience, but also fluidity and grace.

Then there is the linguistic layer. The word **kuàizi** itself is made up of two characters: **Kuài**, meaning *quick*, which is fitting since chopsticks allow nimble, precise movements. **Zi**, meanwhile, is a common noun suffix, often meaning *small thing* or *child*, making **kuàizi**, roughly, *quick little things*. It's a small linguistic window into the practical and playful nature of these utensils.

But this is where it gets complicated, because 'quick sticks' are also *slow* sticks. Psychologically, I think the mastery of chopsticks taps into something deep in the Chinese way of being. It's about patience, control, and mindfulness. You can't rush chopsticks. They demand respect. They demand time. You must focus on the subtle movements of your fingers, the tension between the sticks, and the texture of the food.

In a way, chopsticks are a meditation, a tiny ritual that connects you to centuries of tradition every time you eat. And that is why, for me, chopsticks are one of those things about China that's exactly what you hope it's going to be. They're simple yet profound, frustrating yet rewarding. Every meal is a reminder that you're not just eating food; you're participating in a living culture, one that values connection, history, and the small details of everyday life.

So yes, it took me a long time to get the hang of chopsticks. Yes, there were many embarrassing moments along the way. But now, every time I pick up a morsel of food with my kuaizi, I feel a small victory. A connection. A moment of belonging. Chopsticks encourage a different rhythm and pace to a meal. They slow you down, make you more deliberate. Unlike the aggressive stabbing and cutting of a fork and knife, chopsticks coax you into a more thoughtful relationship with your food. You learn to appreciate each bite, to savour textures and shapes, because you're forced to engage with the food in a tactile way. There's something gentle and respectful about that, and it fits perfectly with the idea that food in China is not merely a fuel but an art form, a social event, a source of identity.

Chopsticks are surprisingly ecological. Unlike the disposable forks and knives common in Western fast-food culture, chopsticks are often made from bamboo—a fast-growing, sustainable resource.

Though China has grappled with issues around disposable chopsticks and deforestation, the tradition itself speaks to a long-standing awareness of nature and resource use. This connection to nature, through the humble chopstick, reflects China's broader, at least historical, respect for harmony between humans and the environment, a theme that reoccurs throughout Chinese philosophy.

I also learned that chopsticks carry symbolic meanings beyond the dining table. In Chinese weddings, newlyweds often receive a set of red lacquered chopsticks as a gift—a symbol of unity, harmony, and the coming together of two lives. The pair of sticks, always used together, represents balance and partnership. Similarly, giving chopsticks as a gift can be a gesture wishing someone good fortune and happy relationships.

Of course, not all chopsticks are created equal.

Across China and East Asia, variations exist. In Northern China, chopsticks tend to be longer and thicker, suited to reaching into large communal dishes. In the south, they tend to be shorter and more tapered, designed for delicate dim sum and fine noodles. Japanese chopsticks are typically more pointed, making them ideal for picking up smaller, bite-sized pieces of food, reflecting differences in cuisine and eating style.

Mastering chopsticks gave me unexpected insights into Chinese social etiquette. For example, when eating with others, it's considered rude to spear food directly onto your plate or to point your chopsticks at someone else. You're expected to take small portions and leave enough for others as a sign of modesty and respect. Certain gestures, like waving chopsticks around or tapping them on the bowl, are discouraged because they signal impatience or disrespect. All these unspoken rules felt like learning a secret code, a way to navigate social harmony through something as simple as how you hold your utensils.

Now, I know what you might be thinking: All this cultural meaning aside, aren't chopsticks just plain annoying when you're hungry and want to eat? And yes, that frustration is real. Even now, after years of practice, I occasionally fumble or drop something. But those small moments of failure only remind me how much I've grown. There's a satisfaction in finally mastering something that once seemed so alien. And it's funny, really, that something so simple can become a badge of cultural belonging.

Eating with chopsticks also changed the way I see food itself. Unlike the Western habit of cutting everything into pieces, chopsticks encourage you to leave food whole or in larger chunks. The idea is to preserve the texture, the bite, the integrity of the ingredient. This led me to appreciate the artistry of Chinese cooking more deeply; the way vegetables are blanched to retain crunch, how meat is sliced thinly but not shredded, and how sauces cling just enough without drowning the dish.

Again, there's a meditation in the small movements of chopsticks. Holding them requires calmness, steadiness, and attention—qualities that stand in contrast to the rushed, distracted world we live in.

I find that chopsticks subtly influence conversation and interaction at the table. Because food is shared, and because chopsticks force you to take only small portions, meals naturally slow down. People eat more mindfully, talk more, and connect more deeply. It's a stark contrast to the typical Western meal, where everyone eats from their own plate, often in silence, wolfing down dinner so they can get back to whatever they deem more important than family time. Eating with chopsticks is a reminder that food is not just nourishment but a social glue.

In the end, chopsticks are one of those magical things about China that meet and exceed your expectations. They're simple yet profound. They're practical yet full of meaning. They're frustrating yet rewarding. They connect you to thousands of years of history, to social rituals, to community, and to the very act of sharing.

So next time you sit down to a Chinese meal, whether in Beijing or your local Golden Dragon, take a moment with your chopsticks. Remember that every tiny motion is part of a story—a dance between past and present, between you and the billions of people who have done the same for centuries. And if you fumble or drop a dumpling? Well, that's part of the fun. Because mastering chopsticks isn't just about skill. It's about connection. It's about patience. It's about being a little less like an outsider and a little more at home.

"I swear to God,
They do it just to keep us out.
They do it just to starve the
Poor little white boy."

– Day 27

Ciqikou

Cíqìkǒu means something like *Porcelain Port*. For those who do not read pinyin, it is pronounced a bit like *tsuh-chee-ko.* The name alone stirs up images of mist curling off a riverbank, of old docks creaking with cargo, of traders in wide sleeves sipping bitter tea and counting silver coins by candlelight. It suggests something delicate, old, and valuable—a fragile holdover from another time.

And that's exactly what I was hoping for when I visited.

Ciqikou is the so-called ancient town nestled in the heart of Shapingba District, the old centre of Chongqing. It's just a short metro ride away, and from the elevated train window, you can see it glowing like a lantern by the Jialing River. From afar, it's magic. Strings of orange light loop across wooden eaves. Red paper lanterns swing above cobblestone alleys. You half expect to see a shadowy scholar with a bamboo fan drifting between the tea houses.

But then you arrive. And when I say *arrive*, I mean *squeeze in*. The crowd hits you like a wall. Not the kind of crowd where you dodge around people and navigate slowly—I mean shoulder-to-shoulder, inch-by-inch human compression. You move when the crowd moves. If the man beside you sneezes, you wear it. If a woman four people ahead drops her phone, it's gone. You are packed so tightly you could be vacuum-sealed.

The first time I went, I was excited. I'd read that Ciqikou was well over a thousand years old, with preserved architecture from the Ming and Qing dynasties. I imagined uneven grey bricks, intricate woodwork, the smell of incense and oolong. What I got was fried squid on a stick and plastic cat ears.

Within five minutes of entering the main street, someone handed me a flier for a bubble tea shop, and someone else tried to sell me a Bluetooth karaoke microphone in neon pink. I passed a noodle shop blasting K-pop and a stall that sold nothing but anime-themed socks. This wasn't an ancient town. It was a theme park without the rides.

Even the buildings, which looked old at first glance, began to crumble under closer inspection—not from age but from lies. The wooden beams were too smooth, the windows too clean. The stone pathways shone with chemical sealant. A friend later told me most of the structures had been rebuilt in the early 2000s to "look traditional"—like when a themed restaurant in Orlando tries to imitate *Ye Olde England* with staff in bonnets and forced 'rustic' decor.

Still, there *are* flashes of authenticity, if you squint. Down a side alley, I once saw an old man with skin like aged leather roasting sunflower seeds in a big iron pan. He didn't speak. Just stirred and roasted, the smell both nutty and comforting. Nearby, a girl played the *erhu*—a two-stringed violin—with surprising grace. Her case was open, a few crumpled notes inside. No speakers, no sales pitch, just music.

But those moments drown in noise. For every quiet courtyard or flicker of old-world charm, there are fifty vendors yelling into megaphones, advertising spicy tofu, or mango drinks, or souvenir panda hats. You're never left alone. You're never given a chance to actually *feel* the place.

But despite all of that, people love it. Local tourists flock there by the tens of thousands. Selfie sticks rise like antennas. Every stone wall becomes a backdrop. Every snack is filmed, chewed, reviewed, shared, and uploaded. It's a site of ritual, a must-see box-tick on your Chongqing visit. And I suppose it serves a purpose. It's accessible, family-friendly, and photogenic. You can tell your friends back home you saw something "cultural" without straying too far from a Starbucks.

But for me, Ciqikou felt hollow. Not just crowded, but *soulless.*

I want to be clear: I have been to other ancient places in China that truly moved me. Towns without entry tickets or LED menus, where elders played mahjong in open courtyards and incense really did curl through the air. Places where the history hadn't been sanded down or dipped in sugar for tourist consumption. In a later chapter, we will delve into Laojundong Temple.

By contrast, Ciqikou was like biting into a wax apple. Perfectly red. Perfectly round. Perfectly tasteless. I went back once or twice, each time hoping it might be different.

Eventually, I stopped trying to see the real China there. Because Ciqikou isn't real. It's a costume. A pretty, curated experience built to satisfy a certain hunger for nostalgia, without the messiness of actual history.

But maybe that's why it's so popular. Ciqikou doesn't ask anything of you. It lets you pretend you've gone back in time, without having to think too hard about what that time was really like. It's history in Instagram form—filtered, marketable, inoffensive. You're free to enjoy it, as long as you don't look too closely. Ciqikou—ancient town, modern trap.

"Ciqikou is to Ancient China
What taxidermy is to the mammoth."

– Day 144

Wide Open Windows in Winter

There are some cultural differences that you can observe from a comfortable distance—like using chopsticks instead of forks, or slurping noodles, or karaoke sessions that begin at midnight and end at dawn. You can smile at them, appreciate them, even adopt them. And then there are other cultural differences that break into your lungs, rattle your immune system, and leave you lying horizontal with a packet of tissues and a mug of boiled ginger water. Wide open windows in winter fall into that second category.

In China, there is a widespread belief that it is healthy—essential, even—to keep the windows open during winter. Not cracked slightly ajar. Not briefly aired in the morning. Wide open. For hours. Sometimes all day.

The idea is that fresh air, no matter how frigid, is better than stale air. That illnesses fester in warm, enclosed spaces. That it's the stagnant air that makes you sick, not the minus temperatures drifting in from the mountains. (I'm not disputing that claim.) But each winter morning, my host mother would march across the living room like a soldier on patrol, push open the windows, and declare: **"Yào tōng fēng!"** (*We must ventilate!*) As if she were banishing a demon. And each winter morning, I'd die a little inside.

The first time I got sick, I blamed the subway. It was logical. The Sky Rail was a daily petri dish of humanity—hundreds of sweaty handles, thousands of mouths breathing recycled air, all pressed together in close, vibrating proximity. So I coughed through it. Tissues, paracetamol, the usual drill.

The second cold came two weeks after the first had ended. This time, I blamed the children I was tutoring—those sweet, snot-nosed six-year-olds. But when the third cold arrived like an unwanted Disney sequel, each one worse than the last, I began to suspect something more elemental. The kind of cold that nestles into your bones and brings you dreams of radiators and double-glazing. That was when I started to notice the windows.

They were always open. Always. The bedrooms, the kitchen, the bathroom. Sometimes they'd even open them on both sides of the apartment to create a perfect wind tunnel, just to make sure no corner was safe from the icy purge.

I tried to protest once, feebly. I gestured to my nose, to my cough, to the goosebumps along my arms. But my host mother just handed me another jacket and said, "You must be more strong."

The windows remained open.

To be fair, they weren't being careless. Quite the opposite—they were being *more* careful than I was. They wrapped up in layers. They boiled everything before eating it. They wore thick indoor slippers and thermal long johns. The windows were open because that's how you stayed healthy. That's how you didn't get sick. That's what their parents had taught them, and their parents before that. Meanwhile, I was shivering on the sofa like a Dickensian orphan.

It wasn't just my host family. Schools kept windows open during lessons. Taxis opened their windows even with the heating on. Restaurants had doors propped open with bricks, as if afraid that warm air might accumulate and form a health hazard. It was as if the entire city was engaged in an unspoken war against insulation.

And I get it—on some level. China is a country that has withstood plagues and fevers. There's a collective memory of disease and how to combat it. Westerners may reach for tissues and rest. In China, you open the windows and drink hot water. It's not that one system is right and the other is wrong—it's that we come from entirely different climates of belief.

But that doesn't mean it's easy to adapt. There are moments in cross-cultural living that test your patience more than others. Not the big things, but the small ones that wear you down. The wet socks on the bathroom floor. The construction at 5 a.m. The food that's too spicy to swallow but which you're too polite to refuse. And yes—those infernal, wide open windows.

I remember one night in particular. The fog had been thick that day. It clung to the city towers, hugging them, enveloping them in a frosty cloak. I was already coming down with a sore throat, the telltale scratch like the notes of an angry violinist. I padded out to the living room in search of tissues, only to find the windows flung open, letting in the kind of wind that feels personal.

I stood there for a long moment, staring at the curtains flapping like sails. Then, very quietly, I closed the window. I slid the latch. I turned around, and my host grandmother was right behind me.

We stared at each other. Me, guilty. Her, puzzled.

"No good," she said gently, and reopened it.

And that was that.

Later, I learned that China's emphasis on ventilation had historical roots. During the SARS outbreak in 2003, keeping windows open became a matter of public health. It worked then, so it became embedded. It's a survival habit, passed down like superstition, until it hardens into common sense. And when Covid-19 came along, it only reinforced that.

So maybe I was the one who needed to adjust. Or maybe some gaps are just too wide to bridge. Either way, I never managed to love the open windows. Not in January. Not in the middle of the night. Not while coughing up the third cold of the season out of my lungs.

Some cultural differences you grow to understand. Some you come to admire. Others you just endure. I'll remember China for its hospitality, its generosity, its endless meals and laughter. But I'll also remember it as the place where I slept in a woolly hat and scarf. It was an experience, for sure, but one that grew old fast. Wide open windows in winter—you will not be missed.

"Too ill to write today.
They're hellbent on giving me the flu
Or hypothermia. Haven't decided which yet."

– Day 215

The Basketball Court

There's a common perception that Chinese kids spend their entire lives buried in textbooks, memorising equations, and re-reading essays. That's not entirely wrong—but it's not the whole picture either. If anything surprised me about life in China, it was how physically active people are. Kids included. Kids most of all! Despite the intense academic pressure, physical health is given the highest level of respect and attention. From an early age, people are expected to move. To stretch. To sweat.

My host family made sure of that. They enrolled me in every sport under the sun... under the big, bright burning sun. Basketball was the main one, mostly because my host brother was obsessed. But I also found myself dragged into games of football, ping pong matches, swimming sessions, and even skiing trips. I'd barely unpacked before someone handed me a badminton racket and pointed to a court.

The basketball court, though—that was where it all happened. It was where I spent most of my time after university, often outmatched by teenagers half my size and twice my speed. At first, I could barely get the ball to hit the backboard. I ran with the coordination of a startled deer. My attempts at dribbling looked like I was trying to stomp out a small fire. And yet, I kept showing up. Not because I was getting any better, but because that's where people gathered. The court was a social hub. Many of my friends were ballers too. After work, young adults would pour in from every direction—ties still half-tied, briefcases flung to the side, a ball bouncing before they'd even done up trainer shoelaces. Old guys sometimes joined in too, sweaty and serious. You'd occasionally see a father in attorney attire toss his jacket to the side and take a few shots before heading home.

Sometimes, we'd play as the sun dipped behind the buildings, the sky a soft, melted, caramelised haze of orange and grey. The streetlights came to life one by one, casting long shadows over the perfectly un-cracked concrete. Music from someone's phone would play hip hop faintly in the background. The sounds of Chongqing—honking horns, scooter engines, crickets chirping—faded into background noise. On the court, time moved differently.

Physical activity wasn't optional. In school, PE was treated with a kind of reverence. There were structured warm-ups, military-style stretches, and timed laps. School uniform was designed with this in mind. Sports were woven into the fabric of childhood, not just as leisure but as part of personal development. It was normal for kids to wake up early for morning drills and stay behind after school for practice. Not just for the top athletes either. Everyone participated in some way.

Health is not just a side concern in China. It's a national priority. Public posters promote daily exercise routines. Elderly people perform coordinated tai chi in the parks at dawn, on every other block. Kids jog around school tracks before first period. Parents invest in physical training with the same zeal as academic tutoring. There are provisions for everything. I played basketball, yes, but also Football on dusty school pitches with no nets. Ping pong in echoey community centres, getting demolished by retirees with terrifying bullet reflexes. Swimming in tiled echo chambers. Skateboarding (badly) at an underground skatepark. Skiing on artificial snow while someone barked instructions in rapid Mandarin. Tennis in the blazing heat. Badminton in a humid gym with zero ventilation.

Some weekends, I had to choose between three or four physical activities, all scheduled by well-meaning adults determined to show me how concerned they were for my health. (In China, people will tell you when you're too fat, or in my case, too skinny.) It was like a buffet of motion. I remember once getting back to the flat, muscles sore, legs trembling, and being asked, cheerfully, whether I wanted to go in goal or midfield; whether I wanted to bat, pitch, or be the shortstop.

It never stopped. There was no time to be still. My weekends filled up before I could object. Even rest felt scheduled. That's what struck me the most: the relentlessness of it all. The drive to always be doing something productive. Improving. Training. Preparing. It made me admire the system, even if I sometimes found it exhausting. These kids were fitter than I ever was at their age. They had better posture, stronger legs, faster reflexes, and they were doing it all while keeping up with schoolwork I could barely understand. Though I have many criticisms when it comes to mental health in China, it is indisputable that a healthy body is one of the first crucial building blocks to a healthy mind.

But there was something else too—something missing. In England, you can spot teenagers hanging around alleyways with nothing much to do. Smoking. Laughing too loudly. Blasting out obnoxious 'music' that can only very liberally be categorised as music. Making bad decisions. (I am being a hypocrite here, but I can say it because I'm in my mid-twenties now). In China, I saw less of that. The streets were clean. The basketball courts were packed. The alleyways were mostly empty. Kids had no time to rebel. They were always on their way to something. Always halfway through a schedule.

That has its upsides. But also, maybe, its costs.

Sometimes I wondered what happened to downtime. To boredom. To the kind of unstructured moments where creativity flourishes. I couldn't remember the last time I'd seen a child just... sit. The kind of loitering that defines Western adolescence—moody silences, spontaneous plans, pointless wandering—seemed absent. Everything had a purpose.

The basketball court became my classroom, not only for sport but for understanding the rhythm of everyday life in China. It was there that I learned how to pass and dribble properly. How to nod instead of speak when you are too out of breath. How to develop thick skin, impermeable to the mocking twelve-year-olds. How to get better by doing, not just watching.

It was also where I noticed just how normal it was to sweat. I know that sounds stupid, but in the West, we're oddly squeamish about exertion. Sweat is treated like something to hide, to be embarrassed by. In China, it was just part of the day. No one flinched if you showed up drenched. If anything, they respected it. There was a kind of dignity in effort. You weren't judged for being bad, only for not trying. I once played a game so terribly that I missed six layups in a row. My teammates didn't laugh. They just told me, "Again," and passed me the ball.

I came to love the basketball court. I even got slightly better. Not good. But better. I stopped missing every shot. I started running without tripping over my own feet. I even managed to win a few games, usually thanks to teammates who carried the weight.

By the time winter rolled around, we were still out there—numb fingers, red ears, visible breath. No one complained. No one asked to stop. It was just what you did.

I realised that health in China wasn't just about policies or facilities. It was about mindset. An expectation that physical fitness matters. That children should be strong, flexible, and agile. Not just smart. Not just polite. And that basketball court, tucked between apartment blocks and trees, became my opportunity to have another crack at these qualities I never mastered in my own childhood.

Since China, I haven't been on a basketball court once, other than to lackadaisically shoot a few half-deflated balls at some hoops. But I have taken up other sports in recent years, sports I'd never taken seriously as a kid, and I believe I have the basketball court to thank for that.

"Arms where my legs should be.
Eyes where my ears should be.
Now I know what it feels like to be
In a Picasso painting."

– Day 163

The 59th Floor

Each floor is a story, each height a chapter in the sprawling novel of urban China.

When I think back on my time in China, I often picture buildings, not just as structures, but as towering monuments to the country's incredible scale and pace of change. Buildings aren't just places to pass through or to sleep in. They are worlds within worlds, layers of life, history, and culture stacked one above another.

I remember three floors in particular: The fifth floor of the *elevatorless* university where I studied Chinese. The thirty-fifth floor of a trade centre, where I wound up getting a tattoo. And the fifty-ninth floor of a residential block, where my host family's great-grandmother lived.

I'll start with the fifth floor of the university. At first, the lack of an elevator felt like a cruel joke. Imagine hauling yourself up steep flights of stairs only to begin a long day of classes, the concrete walls absorbing and radiating the summer heat like a furnace.

But there was something empowering about those steps. It was a kind of daily pilgrimage. Every climb brought me closer to understanding the language, the culture, and the people I had come so far to meet.

On that fifth floor, in a cramped classroom with peeling paint and squeaky fans, I learned the intricate dance of Mandarin's tones—how a slight change in pitch could transform **ma** from mother to horse to scold. I learned how there was a correct and strictly upheld order in which to write the strokes of the characters.

I listened, stumbled, laughed, and slowly gained confidence. That floor became a mountain I had to scale, both physically and metaphorically.

Next: The thirty-fifth floor of a sleazy trade centre, with blackened windows and flickering lights. At eighteen, getting a tattoo felt like a secret rebellion, a rite of passage. From that height, the city stretched endlessly below—streets winding like ribbons, stretching, narrowing, and sprawling down the Yangtze. It was a breathtaking view; one I kept stealing glances at while the artist traced a Siamese fighting fish across my skin. This floor felt less like a climb and more like a threshold between adolescence and adulthood, between being an outsider and becoming a part of the city's pulse.

And lastly, the fifty-ninth floor of a residential block, where I went to meet the family's great-grandmother.

Fifty-nine was almost impossible to fathom. I am fully aware that there are taller buildings across China, across the world, and even in Chongqing. But those hundred-storey buildings are famous. They're celebrated. *This* was just another faceless residential block. One of a number. And on every single floor—one, two, three, four, *all* of them—there was a unique story, and a complex set of lives.

When I looked out of the window, I saw a sea of lights and shapes, an endless muddle of concrete and neon stretching beyond the horizon. People weren't 'ants,' as they say. They were *lice*, and the shorter buildings were merely strands of hair. Dull colours were washed out by brighter colours, only to be dulled again by the fog, the blur-cloud. From up there, the city was a giant brain—every window a synapse, every light a flash of thought, an impulse, a memory, a dream.

To understand why buildings like this exist, you have to grasp the sheer scale of China itself. With a population exceeding 1.4 billion people, almost a fifth of humanity. With a landmass that stretches nearly 3.7 million square miles, but that encompasses deserts, mountains, rivers, and forests, as well as cities. To house such a vast population, urban centres like Chongqing have exploded upwards. Chongqing, often called a 'megacity,' is home to over 30 million people (depending on what you include in the 'urban zone'), which is a population bigger than many countries. It's half the population of England, and most people are oblivious to it! (Locals were certainly shocked to hear that most English people had never heard of Chongqing.)

Chongqing's skyline is a forest of towers. They can't keep building out, and so they build up. Vertical living has become a defining feature of modern Chinese life. Living in a high-rise means sharing space in ways many Westerners like me find surprising. Apartments tend to be compact—often less than thirty square meters for a whole family. Rooms serve multiple purposes: The living room doubles as a dining room, beds have drawers underneath to maximise storage, and furniture folds away to save space.

Elevators are often crowded during rush hours, filled with people carrying groceries, briefcases, or scooters. Walls are thin, meaning neighbours' conversations, radios, and even arguments can be heard clearly. Privacy is more limited than in many

Western homes, and this proximity creates a different kind of community.

Every apartment represents a small universe. Behind each door is a life—a family's joys, struggles, routines, and dreams compressed into a small, vertical space. I often thought about how many stories were layered in the buildings I saw every day. On the fifth floor of my university building, I met students from all over the world—each bringing a piece of their own culture to a shared space. On the thirty-fifth floor of that trade centre, I shared a moment of personal transformation. And on the fifty-ninth floor, I glimpsed an altitudinous life, lived quietly, suspended high above the consciousness of the city.

China's rapid urbanisation means these vertical cities-in-a-city keep rising. Entire neighbourhoods appear and disappear in a matter of months. Cranes dominate skylines, construction workers swarm sites, and steel skeletons rise quicker than a helium balloon.

With so many residents packed in, shared facilities are vital. Laundry rooms, garbage disposal points, communal courtyards, and elevators are lifelines of daily life. In my host family's complex, I saw how residents developed unspoken rules to navigate this closeness. You waited patiently for the elevator, greeted neighbours by name, and shared small courtesies that smoothed the awkward, cramped daily dance.

But living high and tight means sacrifice. Small apartments limit possessions and hobbies. Privacy is a luxury few can afford. Yet, people adapt. They make do.

Visiting the great-grandmother's fifty-ninth-floor apartment was humbling. The elder's simple routine—mornings with tea, afternoons reading newspapers, evenings watching TV—contrasted comically with the overwhelming scale visible from her window.

Looking across at another, almost identical block of flats, forces you to think about other people's lives. It forces you to leave yourself for a moment. All those lives I'd never get to know. All those dreams and fears stacked one above the other, all within my eye-line—all contained, conveniently within my periphery—but still unreachable.

The world you live in is *your* world. The world your neighbour lives in is *their* world. Everyone lives in their own unique world. There are billions of them. You will never know what it's like to live in any of them. Just one. Your own. I realised that no matter how well you know someone, you only ever glimpse a fraction of their story. And in a city of millions, most stories remain hidden behind closed doors. You only get a fragilely thin slice.

The fifty-ninth floor makes you ponder these things. It makes you reflect on your place in an immense city, let alone the universe. Amid such scale, I felt minute. Almost insignificant. I felt powerless. I was both flawed and floored (by the fifty-ninth floor). Not just physically, but emotionally, overwhelmed by the enormity of life around me. Life and death, everywhere. Order and chaos, everywhere. It didn't stop. It didn't notice me, and for the most part, I didn't notice *it*. You can only know so much. Knowledge isn't a fountain.

It's a sea.

But let me return to the ground floor.

The towering buildings symbolise China itself—vast, complex, constantly growing. They remind us that China cannot be understood easily or quickly. Its history, culture, people, and cities are layered and multifaceted. Like the floors of a skyscraper, there is always another level to the madness, another layer to the beauty.

I came to China as a visitor but left feeling like a small part of a much larger whole. The buildings I climbed, the floors I visited, were more than physical spaces; they were lessons in scale, community, and the complexity of life. And the fifty-ninth floor, high above the bustling streets, reminded me that behind every window was a story waiting to be heard. But it likewise reminded me that China, along with the rest of humanity, was a runaway train, hurtling off the tracks, a mind of its own, uncontrollable, unfathomable, and often unscrupulous.

"If I ever had a fear of heights,
It was lost about
Seven hundred floors ago."

– Day 75

Mianzi and Guanxi

There are two words I think you need to know. They're not in any Far East travel guide. They're not written on menus, subway signs, or tourist info brochures. But once you know them, you start to see them everywhere. They float beneath the surface of almost every interaction, like hidden strings tugging gently at the choreography of daily life.

The words are: **miànzi** (*face*) and **guānxì** (*relationship* or *connection*).

Let's start with mianzi.

You may have heard that 'face' is a big deal in Chinese culture, but what you may not realise is just how many faces there are. There's saving face, giving face, losing face, lending face, gaining face, and protecting someone else's face while tactfully disguising the fact that they've just obliterated your own. It's not one concept; it's a whole social ecosystem. It's what holds the spiderweb of politeness, power, obligation, and appearances together.

Let me explain.

It was during my first month in China. My Mandarin was still largely non-existent, my vocabulary half-formed, and I was still at that stage of cultural adaptation where every encounter felt like a cross between a comedy routine and an exam. I'd been invited to lunch by one of the teachers I was working with. She was elegant in that terrifyingly efficient way—immaculate hair, perfect language, eyes that scanned a room like a barcode reader. Her English was good, and so we mostly stuck to English for our conversations, though occasionally she would throw in a Chinese idiom just to confuse me.

We were joined by her husband, a man of few words but endless nods, as well as a local school principal. The principal did not speak English, but that didn't matter, because I was not there to talk. I was there to eat, and to smile, and it turned out, to be tactfully paraded as the school's new foreign acquaintance.

The restaurant was posh, with glass walls, waterfall features, and waitresses who bowed with the precision of ballerinas. I was seated opposite the principal, who poured me tea before I had the chance to pour his, which already put me at a disadvantage. The meal was pleasant, a blur of tofu and small talk. Then came the moment. The teacher offered me a dumpling. A simple act. A kind gesture.

I said no.

"No, thank you," I smiled, in that overly polite British way, still under the delusion that refusing food politely was the proper thing to do.

Her smile faltered. Just slightly. A blink-and-you'll-miss-it moment. The principal glanced at her, then at me. The dumpling hovered in the air, suspended between our chopsticks like a misunderstood handshake.

"You don't like it?" she asked, eyes narrowing ever so slightly.

"No, no, it's not that," I said, waving my hands. "I'm just full."

And that's when I lost face. Not just mine—hers too. I hadn't just refused a dumpling. I had refused a gesture, a role, a moment of harmony. I had disrupted the carefully orchestrated theatre of offering and accepting. In China, when someone offers you something, especially food, especially in a group setting, you're supposed to take it. Even if you're full. Even if you're allergic. You take it, and you smile, and you eat the bloody dumpling.

From then on, I learned. I learned to say yes to things even when I didn't want them. I learned to take the gift, the compliment, the refill, the business card, the responsibility—gracefully, performatively, with the kind of thank-you that carries more than just gratitude.

You see, mianzi is not vanity. It's not ego in the Western sense. It's more like reputation, woven into the moment. It's the difference between winning and appearing to win. Between correcting someone and letting them correct themselves. Between being right and being gracious. I once saw a man refuse to correct the waiter who brought him the wrong dish. He smiled, nodded, thanked the waiter, and ate the whole thing. When I asked him why, he simply said, "I didn't want him to feel bad." That's mianzi. Saving face.

At the same time, mianzi can be a game. It's why meetings start with effusive compliments, why hosts insist on paying for everything, and why the boss gives a speech so long it becomes a second lunch. It's why you sometimes feel like everyone is lying, but no one is lying—everyone is just maintaining the appearance of harmony. No one wants to be the one who breaks the spell.

And then there's guanxi.

If mianzi is the currency of respect, guanxi is the economy itself.

Guanxi is connection. But not the LinkedIn kind. It's not about networking, or schmoozing, or trading business cards with a firm handshake and a smarmy grin. Guanxi is older than that. It's deeper. It's slower. It's relational in a way that Westerners often struggle to understand. Where we might say, "It's not what you know, it's who you know," China would say, "It's who owes you a favour, and who you owe in return."

Because, after all, guanxi is not just a connection. It's an obligation. It's a web of mutual indebtedness that is simultaneously generous and suffocating. Every gift implies a counter-gift. Every kindness, a future return. Guanxi is social credit, long before social credit became an actual government scheme.

Let me tell you about the watermelon.

I was hanging out in a university dormitory at the time, with my two Thai friends and two neighbouring Chinese students. One of the Chinese lads—let's call him *Wei*—knocked on my door holding a watermelon the size of a small child.

"For you," he said.

I blinked.

"I saw you sweating earlier. You said you like fruit. So I got you this."

"That's... wow. Thank you," I said, both touched and confused.

It was not my birthday. There was no occasion. Just a watermelon. A gesture. I accepted it. I thanked him. I tried to give him something in return—a can of Coke or a packet of biscuits—but he waved it off with mock indignation.

"No, no, it's fine. It's just watermelon."

But of course, it wasn't just watermelon. Because two weeks later, he came back. This time with a request.

"I need help with an English essay," he said, grinning sheepishly. "Only three thousand words. Very easy for you."

Now, I'm not suggesting the watermelon was a bribe. It wasn't. It was a seed, planted in the soil of our relationship. And his essay was the fruit. Or possibly another watermelon—I've lost track of the metaphor. But the point is: *That* was guanxi.

In Western cultures, particularly in the UK, we're taught to keep things transactional. Do me a favour, and I'll pay you back. Keep it fair. Keep it clean. In China, guanxi is both messier and more beautiful. It's not about evening the score—it's about building a sense of trust over time. Favour after favour, slowly constructing a relationship that transcends the ledger. This is why guanxi is so powerful. It's how people get jobs, apartments, and school placements. Families are built on it. The lore of generations is conceived in it. It's how problems disappear before they're problems. It's how doors open without knocking. But it's also how nepotism flourishes, how bribes get disguised as generosity, how meritocracy limps behind a convoy of well-connected cousins, nephews, and nieces.

It's also how we got out of a parking fine.

Not for me, obviously—I didn't drive in China. But for the mother of the family. She'd parked her car on a slant, half on the kerb, half in a no-parking zone, outside a furniture warehouse.

When we came out an hour later, there was a bright orange slip on her windscreen. She sighed, dialled a number, and then handed me the phone.

"Just say hello," she said.

"Why?"

"Because it's better if they hear you."

I did as she asked. The man on the other end seemed startled, then amused. He hung up.

"Done," she said.

And just like that, the fine disappeared. Not because of the presence of a foreigner, not really. But because the warehouse owner knew the parking official, and the parking official owed him a favour, and hearing my voice added a novelty factor that made the favour easier to grant.

That's guanxi in action. It's not corruption, exactly. It's lubrication. It's the oil that keeps the gears of society turning, especially in a system where rules are many and loopholes are few. Guanxi is the unofficial fix, the off-menu solution, the back door that's only unlocked if you know the doorman's uncle.

But it's not all favours and flexibility. Guanxi can also be a burden. Because saying 'no' breaks the web. People remember. They remember who said yes. More importantly, they remember who said no.

Which is where guanxi meets mianzi again.

Because if guanxi is the structure, mianzi is the cement. Fulfilling an obligation gives face. Failing to fulfil it takes face away. The entire architecture of society, at least in my limited experience of it, seemed built on these two invisible forces: one structural, the other aesthetic. One political, the other emotional. One gets you in the door, the other keeps you there.

It's also why so much of my time in China felt like a social dance. Every invitation, every compliment, every offer of help carried a second meaning. When someone told me I spoke good Chinese, it wasn't a language assessment. It was a moment of 'face-giving.' When someone refused my money for a service, it wasn't a gift. It was an investment. I was constantly caught between gratitude and suspicion, between appreciation and anxiety that I now owed someone something I hadn't fully understood.

There was one time I tried to be clever. I bought my host family a gift—Scottish shortbread in a decorative tin with tartan ribbon. Hard to find in China, and therefore not cheap. I thought I was being generous. But it backfired. They looked uncomfortable, muttered polite thanks, and placed it immediately in the back of the cupboard at arm's length like an unexploded mine.

Later, I learned why. The gift had been too much. Too expensive. It had created an imbalance. They now owed me face. Worse, they owed me a gift of equivalent or greater value, and I had triggered the arms race of obligation. I'd tried to build guanxi, but instead I'd bulldozed over the subtlety required to do it properly.

Because guanxi isn't built with shortbread. It's built with consistency. With favours small enough to go unnoticed, repeated until they become a rhythm. Guanxi is not about debt. It's about 'relationship as currency.' And relationships, in China, are a kind of infrastructure—just as important as bridges, train lines, or power stations.

The West likes to believe that its relationships are purer. More spontaneous. But the truth is, we have our own versions. We just don't name them. We pretend they're accidental. But if you've ever helped someone move because they once bought you a drink, or if you've ever felt obligated to attend a party you didn't want to go to because they came to yours... that's guanxi. And if you've ever flattered someone at work or stayed quiet to avoid embarrassing someone in public... that's mianzi.

At the end of my time in China, I was given a gift: An antique painting of tall, steep hills, clouds, and calligraphy—I suspect it was meant to be the national park of Zhangjiajie. It was beautiful. Generous. And despite everything I've said, I knew without a doubt that this gift was just that. A gift. Heartfelt and innocuous. It expected nothing in return. It wasn't an opening move—not a gambit—but a conclusion. A graceful ending.

Mianzi and Guanxi are very real, but they're the natural extremes of such a wonderfully munificent culture. Let's not be too quick to judge.

"It is I for whom the phrase:
'You'll have to forgive him; he's not from around here'
Was conceived."

– *Day 166*

The Mass Nap

There are countries where napping is considered a luxury. And then there's China, where napping is a necessity—a biological rebellion staged in silence, bar the occasional snore, every single day after lunch.

The first time I walked through a Chinese office at midday, I thought I'd stumbled into the aftermath of some kind of gas leak. Desks were abandoned mid-email. Chairs were tilted at odd, sleep-optimised angles. People were draped over tables and curled beneath windowsills like the dolls of a child who doesn't know how to tidy up after playtime. A woman was slumped forward in a desk chair with a scarf over her eyes—a blindfolded statue. A man was snoring gently in the corner, limbs tangled in a suit and tie—a forgotten marionette.

It looked like a corporate apocalypse.

And yet, no one was alarmed. I wasn't intruding. I wasn't late. I was just *awake*, in a place where wakefulness had been temporarily suspended. A whole office floor had folded itself into a collective sleep. The buzz of air conditioning became the only sign of life. Computers hummed. Sleep reigned.

The midday nap—**wǔxiū**—is an extremely Chinese phenomenon, though one that surprised me at first. The mass midday nap is a shared agreement between the employers, the employees, and the lunch bell. People sleep wherever they are. At desks. On cardboard mats. In chairs pushed together like puzzle pieces. Heads cradled in the crook of an elbow or cushioned by a plastic lunchbox lid. Of course, I'm not naive enough to think all workers are able to benefit from this, but it's a lot more common than you'd think in such a hard-working country like China.

It happens in schools. In restaurants. In corner shops where the cashier disappears behind a hanging curtain and you're left staring at a till with no operator. It's not laziness. It's not a lifestyle choice. It's practically survival.

Because the truth is, people in China are *tired*. Full of energy, yet tired. It's a paradox. This is a country that runs long. School days that start at seven and end after dark. Work hours that bleed into home hours. Homework that makes British syllabuses look like doodling. Parents who come home only to start their second shift—teaching, feeding, preparing, worrying.

Even the elderly don't rest. I've seen grandmas with toddlers strapped to their backs, weaving through markets with six bags of vegetables in one hand and a phone to their ear in the other. I've seen men in their sixties welding scaffolding barefoot in the sun, then sitting down for a ten-minute nap on a cement bag before standing up and carrying on.

There's a term in China: **Jiǔ jiǔ liù** (*nine-nine-six*). It means working from 9 a.m. to 9 p.m., six days a week. It's become shorthand for the country's grind culture, especially in tech companies and private firms. Officially, it's illegal. In 2021, China's Supreme Court ruled that 996 violates labour laws. But like so many things in China, the law and the lived reality often exist in parallel universes. Off the record, from what I understand, it's still common. Quietly endured. Widely expected. Sometimes even framed as a badge of honour—proof that you're loyal, hungry, willing to sacrifice. Other times, it's just silently suffered through, a schedule that eats your week whole and spits out your weekends in fragments. So when lunch hits, and the rice boxes are scraped clean, and the hot water has cooled, the nap begins.

I once visited a friend in a towering office block in Chongqing. It was around 12:40. I pressed the wrong lift button and exited one floor early. When the doors slid open, I thought I'd entered a squat or a crime scene. Shoes were kicked off. Jackets had been folded into makeshift pillows. A man was lying flat beneath his desk, phone in hand, watching an old TV drama on mute as he drifted off. Another had pulled two office chairs together and straddled them like a defeated cowboy. One woman had climbed onto the windowsill and curled up like a cat in a sunbeam.

Not a single light was on. Just the faint blue glow of sleeping laptop screens and the dusty wash of midday light filtering through greyed glass.

At first, I found it amusing. Then charming. Then quietly devastating. Because once you realise how unavoidable the nap is, you start to see it for what it is—not a luxury, but a last-ditch effort to be human in a system that eats hours whole.

I've seen naps like this elsewhere: *La siesta* in Spain, *Il riposo* in Italy. But this was different. This wasn't time off work to deal with Mediterranean heat. This was time *at* work to deal with mental, physical, and *spiritual* fatigue.

There's something tragic about people asleep on hard tables, arms folded, necks bent at angles that would make any half-decent physiotherapist cringe. Some keep neck pillows in drawers.

Some bring tiny blankets. Others just fold their jacket over their face and disappear.

And then, 1:30 hits.

People wake like a forest of spring-loaded scarecrows. They rub their eyes, sip thermos tea, and return to Excel spreadsheets without a word (apart from the Microsoft kind). There's no stretching. No sighing. Just the silent machinery of life cranking back into motion.

Once, I tried to join them. Of course I did. The foreigner always does. We want to blend in. We want to 'when in Rome' it. I laid my arms across the desk, nestled my forehead into a hoodie, and willed myself to sleep. Nothing. My mind wouldn't cooperate. It was buzzing—*Is this allowed? Am I pretending? Do I look weird? Should I be doing something productive? Is this productive? Is someone watching me?* And so on. Meanwhile, everyone else was fully unconscious. It wasn't a gimmick for them. It wasn't a holiday perk. It was a physical surrender. A mass yielding to fatigue. And not just fatigue from the day—but from months, years, lifetimes of hard work and impossible expectations.

Eventually, I stopped trying to nap. But I never stopped watching. There's a strange intimacy to watching a city sleep during the day. You catch people unguarded, slack-jawed, fingers twitching, shoulders soft. In a culture that often values restraint and formality, the nap is a quiet dismantling of the mask. It's one of the few times when one is simply a body. Not a teacher. Not a manager. Not a mother, student, or bureaucrat. Just a tired human being, trusting the clock to wake them up before things fall apart.

I began to think of the mass nap as a kind of unofficial protest. Not loud. Not political. Just insistent. Sleep as the only break left. Not because life is leisurely, but because it's *too much*. Sleep as the last private act in a life that's scheduled, counted, and measured in deliverables.

Perhaps what struck me most was that no one ever questioned it. You don't need permission to nap. No one rolls their eyes or mutters the word 'lazy' under their breath. The act is so embedded, so institutionalised, that it becomes invisible. Like breathing. Like blinking.

In the UK, if you fall asleep at work, you're either unwell, depressed, or about to be sacked. In China, it just means it's 12:45. And you don't have to be comfortable. You just have to be still. You just have to close your eyes, even for twenty minutes, and offer yourself back to your body, to your brain, to whatever weary part of you has been carrying the load all morning.

I saw people nap through building drills, mosquito swarms, and printer malfunctions. I saw a man fall asleep standing up, leaning against a metal road sign. I saw a woman nod off mid-conversation, apologise, and carry on talking.

It taught me something. About limits. About kindness. About quiet survival. Because this wasn't laziness. It wasn't slowness. It was the rhythm of a population that runs hard, and fast, and long—and needs that one moment of collapse to keep going. It was a nation catching its breath.

For all its awkwardness, its oddness, its improvised pillows and stiff necks, I came to look upon the mass nap with sympathetic admiration. At least it was true, honest, and real. People are tired. And they nap. Together.

"It reminds me of a game we used to play in primary school. 'Sleeping lions.' Except no one in here is pretending."

– Day 208

Vomiting, Nausea, and Fingertip Needles

(Content warning: Vomiting, blood, needles.)

It began at 4:03 a.m., which I remember with such precision because I was recording the time between retches. There's something profoundly humbling about vomiting. It strips you of any pretence. There's no dignity in it—just you, gravity, and a body that has decided it has had enough. In my case, *far* more than enough. I vomited so hard and for so long that I began to wonder if I might run out of stomach lining.

It wasn't food poisoning. At least, I don't think it was. I had eaten hot pot the night before, which in Chongqing could be considered a risky move on the best of days. But I was used to it. I'd been in China for months by this point. I'd eaten tentacles, chicken feet, and mystery noodles slurped from plastic bags. I had survived the street food stalls, and the tap water warnings, and even a fermented tofu incident that still makes me shudder. But that morning, something in my body revolted. It felt less like illness and more like a full-scale rebellion.

I should explain at this point that I have a complicated and largely undiagnosed autoimmune disorder that seems to manifest differently each year. At the time, it took the form of intense abdominal migraines, diarrhoea, and vomiting.

My host dad, who had been fast asleep on the other side of our paper-thin wall, sprang into action with all the concern and decisiveness of a battlefield medic. Within thirty minutes, I was bundled into the back of his car, clutching a plastic bowl like a life raft. I asked which hospital we were going to.

He looked back and said, regretfully, "**Er jí yīyuàn**."

Second-class hospital.

In China, hospitals are categorised like hotels. There is a healthcare system, but the rich have access to better hospitals. But that night we were staying in the lower-city apartment, and the nearest hospital, by far, was of the second-class kind. A place where, if your illness didn't kill you, the facilities might.

The hospital was like something from a war zone. Outside, people milled around on the steps, some sitting on IV drips attached to their own portable metal stands, as if they had checked themselves in and were now waiting for someone to remember they existed. A man was lying flat on a cardboard mat. I wasn't sure if he was sleeping or dying. A dog with matted fur trotted past the reception. The walls were yellowed with time, or nicotine, or possibly both. Signs hung at crooked angles. The queue snaked into itself. I wasn't in a position to analyse it all carefully because I had begun vomiting again—into the same bowl that had now become a semi-permanent extension of my hands (or rather, my *stomach*). It was nearly overflowing.

Eventually, after negotiations at the front desk and some pointing at my passport, we discovered that the department I needed to visit was on the fourth floor. But the elevator, predictably, was broken.

It's hard to describe the exact sensation of climbing three flights of stairs while projectile vomiting, but I'll try: Imagine someone slowly turning your entire insides into a washing machine, while gravity punches you in the gut every four steps. That just about covers it.

By the time I reached the fourth floor, I was hunched like a wounded animal. They led me to a chair and gestured that I needed a blood test. *Fine,* I thought. *Just get it over with.* I'm no stranger to blood tests. Or so I thought. But I wasn't prepared for what followed. The nurse—who didn't look particularly thrilled to see me—grabbed my hand and stabbed a needle vertically into the very tip of my index finger. Not the side. The tip. Right where every nerve ending in the human body lives, evidently.

Of course, I was eighteen and 'cool,' so I didn't yelp, and I didn't moan, and I definitely didn't cry. But something had to come out, so I laughed hysterically.

But then came the worst part: the squeezing. Because the blood was sluggish—perhaps because I had already expelled every available fluid in my body—they had to extract it manually. She began kneading the finger like she was trying to juice a stubborn lemon—seeds and all. My entire hand went pale. I watched the blood slowly pool into a tiny plastic cylinder.

I was already nauseous, but this tipped me over. Something about the whiteness of my skin, the pinprick of pain, the dark red life-sustaining liquid leaking from me drop by drop; it all combined into a wave of de-oxygenating dizziness that made me hunch over the bin beside me.

And then I threw up again.

There's a kind of loneliness that comes from being sick in a country where you don't speak the language fluently. You can't explain your symptoms. You can't ask the right questions. You can't tell them your allergies or your medical history. You're reduced to miming your pain and hoping someone understands—the best part is when the medical professionals join in with the game of charades. But even when they do understand the problem, the system itself might not be equipped to help you.

China's healthcare system is complicated, and not always in a good way. Hospitals in China operate differently from many Western countries. You don't just show up at A&E and wait to be seen. Instead, you register at the front, pay a small fee for a consultation (because almost every interaction costs something), and then wait to be assigned to a doctor. Most hospitals are overcrowded, especially in cities. Doctors see dozens of patients per hour. Privacy is unheard of. You might get diagnosed while five other people are standing around, listening in. And they'll talk about everything. Loudly. Your blood pressure, your salt levels, your deficiencies, your urine colour, your stool consistency, your deepest insecurities—out loud, in front of a crowded room like it's a spectator sport.

And while the system *can* be efficient in some ways—medication is usually handed to you within minutes—there are serious cracks in the foundation. Urban hospitals are overwhelmed. Rural ones are underfunded. Access to care is not equal. And corruption, though less overt than it once was, still lingers like the smell of fireworks on the 6th of November.

I was lucky. I had someone advocating for me—my host dad, who stayed by my side the entire time, missing his morning commute to work, frowning at paperwork, arguing with receptionists. Without him, my night could have gone very differently. I told him sorry so many times. I kept saying it over and over again. **Duìbùqǐ, duìbùqǐ, duìbùqǐ**... But he didn't seem to understand why I was apologising. I guess I was apologising because where I came from, that's just what you did. But more than that, I was deeply embarrassed and scared, and **duìbùqǐ** became something of a comfort word.

I won't go into details about what I had to go through in the hospital, because I don't see any value in that. But while I was lying there, I remember thinking, *This is what healthcare feels like when it's stretched to the brink.*

And China isn't alone in this.

In America, healthcare is a luxury. It's tied to employment, or insurance, or luck. You can be bankrupted by a broken arm. Ambulances cost hundreds. A friend once told me he had to "shop around" for hospitals, like it was a pair of new shoes. He got a quote for his emergency surgery—*a quote*. As if medical intervention were a wedding cake or new bathroom floor tiling.

Back home, in the UK, we have the NHS—a marvel in many ways but one currently wheezing under the weight of mismanagement and sheer numbers. Waiting lists are months long. Some services are desperately underfunded. And while it's free at the point of use, it's often a long and painful road to actually *get* that use, for some more than others. Sometimes, by the time the system gets around to seeing you, you no longer need help, or the issue is much worse, or you're dead.

So I'm not saying China is uniquely flawed. What I am saying is, being ill anywhere reminds you of how fragile these systems are. And being ill in China—especially as a foreigner—teaches you that resilience doesn't always come from the body. Sometimes it comes from the people around you, or from your determination to keep walking upstairs even when everything in you wants to collapse.

Later that evening, after the worst had passed, my host dad took me home and cooked me congee, white rice porridge, bland and comforting. Plus a cup of hot water—always hot water. He sprinkled the congee with spring onion or something and set it beside my bed. I could barely eat it, but I remember the gesture.

It meant something. He didn't speak much English, but in that moment, he didn't need to.

I think about that hospital often. About the dirty walls and the barking, flea-ridden dogs and the blood being squeezed from my finger like a toothpaste tube. I think about how vulnerability changes depending on where you are. In some places, it's economic. In others, linguistic. Sometimes it's just the damn elevator.

It's not a particularly inspirational story. There's no neat conclusion, no lesson about bravery or endurance. Just a quiet, aching truth: Getting sick abroad is shit. It's terrifying. Not that it's particularly pleasant in your *home* country. But surviving it gives you a new kind of empathy for everyone who has ever had to navigate a broken healthcare system while holding their insides together with sheer willpower.

There are people in China and across the world who have *no* access to healthcare, with much worse conditions than mine. There's nothing I can do about that, and in a way, that terrifies me much more than anything I have had to endure.

"I'm a day late writing today.
Long story. I'd quite like to forget it anyway.
I need to go get some fresh air."

– Day 94

3-Wheeled Little Bouncy Thing

It was late. I was tired. There was a long hill ahead of me. Miles long. I had a backpack full of heavy textbooks to lug. I needed a taxi, so I hailed one of the many yellow cabs and told the driver where I needed to be.

"Can I just check how much it will cost?"

"About fifteen renminbi."

Thank God, I thought. *That's nothing.*

I looked in my wallet only to find I had nothing left. Ten yuan to my name. As usual, my credit card had stopped working. (Miraculously, I lived mostly on cash in China.) Embarrassed, I told him I didn't have the money. He shook his head, muttered some curse in Chongqinghua, and drove off. It was impossible for some locals to believe that a white person had 'run out of money.'

I thought about sleeping on a bench... that's how tired I was. But then I remembered something. **Sān bèng zi!**

I'm not entirely sure how it translates. Something like "three-wheeled little bouncy thing." Just like hospitals were tiered in China, so was transport. If you couldn't afford a yellow cab, you could probably afford a three-wheeled, rattly, noisy electric mule, usually driven by an old guy without a license. (Incidentally, I hear that China has been cracking down on them recently. I'm not even sure how easy it would be to find one anymore. But at the time, they were everywhere.)

I walked up to one, startling the guy inside, who was cutting through a banana skin with his teeth. He was wearing a straw hat like in the movies.

"How much?" I asked.

"You want to go up hill? Six."

He held out his hand, spreading his thumb and pinkie finger out like a pretend phone. In China, that was the hand symbol for six. (They have hand symbols for the numbers, which I quite miss. They meant you could barter in noisy markets without needing to open your mouth.)

I gave him ten and told him to keep it as long as he could get me up the hill. He grinned with his three remaining teeth and shuffled over to make room. I climbed in, clutching my backpack, which immediately slid off the narrow seat and wedged itself somewhere between a loose battery casing and a plastic water bottle filled with what I hope was apple juice.

The thing sputtered to life like a dying lawnmower. It didn't drive so much as judder, rattle, and snarl its way forward. Within seconds, we were bouncing down the road at warp speed. It was like riding a jackhammer strapped to a shopping cart. The metal frame shook so violently I thought one of my kidneys might fall out. I tried to hold on to something, anything. But there were no seatbelts, just rusty, windowless window frames.

We swerved into traffic without warning. No indicator, no check over the shoulder; just pure confidence and inertia. Cars honked, pedestrians leapt out of the way. At one point, we launched off the road and up onto the pavement, narrowly missing a woman pushing a pram and a guy deep in a phone call. My driver seemed wholly unconcerned. He was humming a tune and spitting bits of banana skin out the window.

I tried not to look at the speedometer, which was either deceitful or painfully honest. We hit a pothole the size of a turtle, and the entire cabin lifted a few inches off the base with a *CLANG*. My teeth clicked together like castanets.

At one point, I think we drove through a construction site. The driver knew routes that respectable cab drivers refused to venture down. Somewhere in the chaos, I completely lost my sense of direction. Everything vibrated. All I could hear was that constant metallic scream coming from the undercarriage. And then, miraculously, we made it. He skidded to a stop with a cheerful "**hǎo le!**" and looked back at me as if to say, *Wasn't that fun?*

I staggered out, legs shaking, backpack digging into my shoulder, my brain still rattling around. But I was home. Or close enough. I turned back to wave at the driver. He grinned with bits of banana between his teeth and waved goodbye.

"Today I rode a three-wheeled, little bouncy thing.
I think I have a concussion, and my vision is still blurred.
Best ten yuan I ever spent."

– Day 138

Temporary Lower-Body Paralysis

There was no warning. Just a ‘polite’ suggestion over breakfast.

“You’re folding in on yourself,” my host mother said, ladling thick rice porridge into my bowl. “Your back is like noodles.”

I looked up, mid-chew.

“I’m not sure what to say.”

“We will go and fix it,” she said, ominously.

That afternoon, she sent me to an acupuncture clinic. Not for an injury. Not for stress. Not even for pain. For slouching. In all honesty, my back *had* been aching terribly, but there was no way *she* could have known that—was there?

The clinic was tucked behind a chemist’s counter, squeezed between a shoe shop and a place that sold only electric fans. It smelled like old menthol and stewed socks. Inside, the lights were bright and buzzing, the floor tiles yellowed with time. A thin man with tired eyes demanded that I lie down and take off my shirt. He didn’t introduce himself.

Just said, “Cups first.”

Cupping. I’d heard of it. I was expecting to be relaxed, not sucked up into a glass bowl like lint going up a Hoover! In case you don’t know about cupping, he basically lit small fires in glass jars, then flipped each one onto my back with practised rhythm. Within seconds, my skin was being dragged upward—flesh and muscle sucked into warm vacuums that made loud, obscene pops. I could feel my back bubbling like a hot pot. Ten, twelve, fifteen cups. It was hard to count. It didn't hurt, but it wasn't pleasant either. More like an odd, deep itch that you couldn't scratch because you were being swallowed by glass octopuses.

The man left the room. I lay there alone, fused to the table like some specimen in a science museum: The Slouching Foreigner, preserved in a jar... in cups.

Eventually, he returned and pulled them off. I wish there were an arrangement of letters that could accurately recreate the sound, but this is the closest I've got: *Squelch. Squelch. Squelch.*

I flinched each time.

Then he began the acupuncture, and I wished I'd saved my flinching for this procedure instead. You imagine acupuncture as a delicate thing—maybe a light tickle, something holistic and graceful, like someone tuning a harp made of your spine.

Not this guy.

He held the needles between his fingers like he was sewing sails. No ceremony. Just stab, stab, stab, down the length of my back, pressing them deep into unknown, uncharted territory. The final one went straight into the base of my spine. Something in me went dark. I tried to move. Nothing. My legs, which had been happily attached to my body moments before, were now distant relatives. There was no pain. Just absence. I couldn't twitch a toe, couldn't even send the signal to do so.

For the first ten seconds, I thought: *That's interesting.* By twenty seconds: *This seems... not great, to be honest.* At thirty seconds: *OK, I'm paralysed. I'm paralysed, and I'm arse-naked, and I'll probably die here. He's checking his phone. Why's he checking his phone? Is he looking for medical advice?*

I opened my mouth to speak but didn't. British instinct. I didn't want to be rude. Or dramatic. Or interrupt his research. Perhaps he knew what he was doing. Or perhaps this was how I lived now.

Time passed slowly. My thoughts bounced around in circles. How many needles are in me right now? Am I allowed to scream?

Turns out he'd just been on the phone with his daughter-in-law. That's what he told me. And then, wordlessly, one by one, he plucked the needles out, like he was harvesting tiny metal radishes from the world's most anxious garden. And then... sensation. First pins and needles. Then warmth. Then legs. Real, responsive legs. I stood. Slowly. Wobbled. Breathed.

That's when I realised how incredible I felt. My spine was awake. My shoulders, for the first time in years, weren't trying to kiss each other. I had *posture*. I was standing at least two inches taller. I was also breathing deeper, into pulmonary depths I didn't know I had. My shadow looked elongated, like in the evening sun, except it was midday.

I floated out of the clinic like a confessor who had shed sin and spine curvature in one miraculous session.

I ran into my host mother on the way home.

She looked me up and down.

"Good," she said. "No more noodle boy."

I wanted to be insulted, but I really quite enjoyed being 'no more noodle boy,' and so I rolled with it.

That night I looked at my back in the mirror. Red rings bloomed across it like angry crop circles. But inside? Lighter. Calmer. Realigned.

I never went back. I should have. I still should. Every so often, I feel my neck tightening again, my shoulders slinking forward, my spine beginning to coil into that familiar guilty question mark. Especially since I found out the mattress I've been using for years is only intended for 'temporary use.'

I think about that man, and his needles. I think about that moment of total paralysis. The terror. The trust. The transformation. I think it's probably time for another cupping. Overall, I am grateful for the experience of Chinese acupuncture and temporary lower-body paralysis.

"Later on, I'm going to some kind of
Physiotherapy or something for my back.
Shouldn't be too bad."

– Day 233

The Moped Family of 4

The first time I truly considered my mortality in a moving vehicle was on the Chengyu Expressway, heading out of the city in the late afternoon. The mother sat up front, the father was at the wheel, and between them—on the armrest, no seatbelt, no helmet, no nothin'—sat their two-year-old, happily chewing on a packet of dried fruit as if he wasn't currently auditioning for the new *THINK!* advert.

We seemed to be doing main-road speeds out of the driveway, motorway speeds on the main roads, and intergalactic speeds on the motorway. To a Western eye, the scene is shocking. In Britain, you can be fined for having the wrong type of booster seat. In China, I saw a toddler effectively moonlighting as an extra gearstick.

Once you start noticing it, you see it everywhere. The casual physics-defying transport arrangements of Chinese families. Parents riding electric mopeds with one child balanced on the handlebars and another clinging to their back. Teenagers doubled up on a single seat, legs dangling like mismatched curtain tassels. The most I've personally counted is five people on a single moped—an entire nuclear family and a plus-one on two wheels.

At first, you think: *That can't possibly be safe.* Then, you think: *That can't possibly be comfortable.* Eventually, you just nod to yourself and think: *Well, that's one way to beat rush hour.*

It's not that Chinese people don't care about safety—it's that the cultural approach to it feels entirely different. In the West, we pad, and strap, and reinforce until our children are encased like high-security parcels. In China, especially in smaller cities or rural areas, there's more trust in balance, instinct, and sheer stubborn will. It's as if the unspoken philosophy is: *We've been doing it this way for decades, and most of us are still here.*

Part of it comes down to infrastructure. Many families don't own a car, and even if they did, parking is a nightmare in most Chinese cities. Mopeds are cheap, fast, and can snake through traffic in ways that cars can only dream of. Public transport is fantastic for longer distances, but for quick trips to the market or school, the moped reigns supreme. If you've got four pairs of legs and only two wheels, you improvise.

There's an undeniable elegance to it. The driver leans into a turn, the passengers adjust their weight instinctively, and somehow, miraculously, everyone stays upright. I used to watch families pull away from traffic lights with a kind of enjoyment, as though they were a single organism: four hearts, sixteen limbs, one shared sense of balance.

That's not to say it's entirely without consequences. The WHO's road safety statistics for China are sobering, and hospitals in every province see their fair share of roadside victims. The year before I went to China, my cousin died in a car crash, and so seeing these Newton's-Third-Law-defying manoeuvres didn't impress me; they made me upset.

The first few weeks, I was constantly on edge. Every honk felt like a warning of imminent doom, every sudden swerve a prelude to a crash. But over time, something strange happened. I stopped gripping the seat so tightly. I stopped bracing at every lane change. I even stopped praying. The chaos began to feel like a system—messy, yes, but a system all the same.

It's tempting to frame all of this as a metaphor for life in China: crowded, fast-moving, occasionally reckless, but somehow holding together through inertia, momentum, and mutual awareness. On the back of a moped, you are part of a living tide, everyone trusting that the person in front will make the right split-second decision, and that you will, too. There's no room for hesitation.

One evening, I saw a moped pull up next to me at a set of traffic lights. The driver was a young man, maybe mid-twenties. Behind him sat a woman cradling a baby, the tiny head just visible in the crook of her arm. Wedged between them, holding on to both adults, was a little girl of about ten. The baby was sleeping, the girl was grinning, and the parents were chatting like they were on a park bench, not idling in the middle of an intersection. Not a helmet in sight, of course. When the lights turned green, they pulled away in one fluid motion—the driver's left hand steady on the handlebars, his right adjusting the baby's blanket without missing a beat. It was terrifying. It was beautiful. It was China.

I still don't know whether my comfort level surrounding this matter grew from genuine trust or simple repetition. You can't live in a constant state of panic; your body finds a way to adapt. By the end of my stay, I could ride through the centre of Chongqing in rush hour without feeling my pulse spike. I could even appreciate the strange harmony of it all.

Of course, now that I'm back in the UK, I automatically buckle my seatbelt before the ignition is even on. Old habits reassert themselves quickly. But sometimes, when I'm sitting in traffic, inching forward in an orderly queue of samey, regulated hatchbacks, saloons, and SUVs, I remember the moped family of four. The wind in their hair. The grin on the little girl's face. The unspoken agreement between rider, passenger, and the chaos around them. But normally, I shake my head free of such thoughts and buckle the hell up. Armrests are for paper coffee cups and... well, *arms*. Not toddlers.

"You know that little grab handle
On the passenger side of most cars?
I know what it's for now—
China."

– Day 68

Covid-19

The first time I heard about it, I was playing basketball. It came to us in a gentle whisper from across central China. It drifted southwest like tumbleweed. At first, we thought nothing of it. It didn't have a name yet. Just another flash of some faraway news that had nothing to do with us, like lightning on the horizon. Sort of scary, but rendered small and unimportant by distance.

"Did you hear about Wuhan?" asked a friend of mine, sweeping the ball under his legs.

"No, what do you mean?"

"There's this... what is it called in English?" He aimed for the hoop and missed. "Like when you are very ill, and it goes all over the city."

"A virus?" I guessed, retrieving the ball.

"Virus. Yes. In Wuhan."

His older brother laughed from the edge of the court and said, "Virus come all time. Virus go."

That was true, I thought. Virus come. Virus go.

A week later, it wasn't just Wuhan anymore. The whisper had become a chant, and then a warning siren. It was everywhere: On TVs in noodle shops, in every message group, on LED banners scrolling across bus stops. It was no longer a rumour from far away; it had a name now. Suddenly, everyone was talking virology. People who had once told me they'd never left Chongqing were now tracing theoretical disease vectors on their fingers over a paper map of China.

My host mum, a woman who usually gave me wisdom about herbal leaves and good qi, had started handing out gossip about airborne transmission and the correct angle at which to wear your face mask.

You could feel it in the air. Something had changed. People were buying masks the same way they used to buy fresh vegetables. The pharmacies were sold out. The street markets, once a daily flood of voices, grew strangely quiet. Even the taxi drivers, who never stopped talking, had gone silent behind their surgical blue masks.

Lockdown came not with a bang, but with a bow. At first, it was polite. Encouraging. Government messages reminded people to stay home, to protect their families, to keep warm, and to wash their hands. Posters showed smiling cartoon characters wearing masks. It felt like a public health campaign with a cheerful tone.

Then it got real.

Roads closed. City borders shut. QR codes appeared at every doorway like digital gatekeepers. You needed a health code to walk into a shop or catch a bus. Some apartment buildings padlocked their entrances. In Chongqing, where the streets ran like vertical arteries, the silence was especially surreal. No traffic. No shouting. Just the distant cough of an idling motorbike or a lone delivery driver wheeling food to a block of flats.

And the police were everywhere. Not threatening. Not loud. But present. Quietly watching. Wearing reflective jackets and disposable gloves, their expressions unreadable behind the fabric of their masks. (I'm sorry to say it, but it reminded me of stormtroopers in *Star Wars*.) The Chinese flag fluttered behind them. If you strayed too far or didn't have the right code on your phone, they'd politely—but firmly—redirect you.

The discipline of the public was staggering. One day, the entire city was a writhing knot of 8D roads, and street food stalls, and people shouting into their phones while they crossed six lanes of traffic. The next day, order. Stillness. Collective obedience. It wasn't fear, exactly. It was something else. A shared understanding. This wasn't just *your* problem—it was *ours*.

China has a complicated relationship with control. On one hand, it's a nation of 1.4 billion people who largely believe in collective strength, duty to family, and the power of government to organise chaos. On the other hand, it's full of people who precariously jaywalk like it's an Olympic sport, who gamble behind shop counters and sell knock-off Gucci from the back of vans. It's a country that contains both rule-followers and the most creative loophole-exploiters I've ever met.

But when Covid came, the pendulum swung hard toward obedience. Even the rebels played along. Even the gamblers went home. Everyone—taxi drivers, merchants, students—stayed indoors.

In the spirit of full disclosure, Covid-19 came towards the end of my time in China, and I was lucky enough to have escaped on what might have been the last plane out of Beijing International Airport. (Before you speculate, I was not one of the so-called 'superspreaders' who brought the virus to the rest of the world. The first time I tested positively for Covid-19 was years later.)

When I arrived back in London, it was like the virus had been a bad dream. No one in Europe seemed interested, and for a while, I started to think it was merely an overreaction of the

Chinese government. I even briefly questioned whether it was in fact real. It wasn't until weeks later that my country started to take it more seriously.

But I continued to monitor the situation. My Chinese friends had all become dependent on their phones, not just for news and communication, but for permission. The health code system—**jiàn kāng mǎ**—became a kind of digital passport. It showed green if you were safe, red if you weren't. Where you had been. Who you'd come into contact with. It was a matrix of surveillance and reassurance.

So where did the virus come from?

They said it started in a wet market in Wuhan. From an animal. A bat, maybe. Or a pangolin. The virus jumped species and entered the bloodstream of a densely packed urban population. From there, it exploded outward. That's the mainstream theory. But in China, there were other theories. Some said it came from America, that US soldiers brought it during the military games. Others whispered that it was a lab leak, that it didn't *escape* so much as *emerge*—carefully, or carelessly, depending on your politics.

These weren't just tinfoil-hat conspiracy theories. They were real conversations happening in taxis, on WeChat, in quiet corners of tea shops. Everyone had a theory. Few completely trusted the official story. But at the same time, few pushed too hard. That's how it works: You question, but only so far. You speculate, but then you return to your place in the pattern.

Covid-19 taught me things about China that I had seen little of in the many months prior. It showed me the power of the Chinese state—to coordinate, to track, to isolate, to mobilise. In the West, this kind of mass shutdown would be fought tooth and nail. But in China, it just... happened. And fast. That efficiency was both impressive and frightening. It was the kind of control that made you feel safe, and also frightfully unsafe.

It showed me something else as well about the resilience of the people. I saw it in the way grandmothers figured out how to scan QR codes and order groceries online. In the way students switched to online classes with minimal complaint. In the way neighbours left spare masks hanging on each other's doors.

There were cracks too, of course. Not everyone trusted the data. Some people quietly defied curfews. And there was fear—fear that wasn't always spoken aloud but lived in the corners of people's eyes.

For me, Covid-19 was the end of my time in China. It briskly shut the door behind me and locked it from the inside. I had spent months inadvertently building a life there—imperfect, chaotic, beautiful—and it ended in silence, blue masks, and QR codes.

It killed billions of plans. It ended love stories, job opportunities, and ideas. It made us all cautious. But it also made us remember. Remember how small we are. How connected we are. How quickly everything can change. The virus gave us many things, from death to fear to the severing of connections. But it also gave us a lesson about governments, about ourselves, and about the air between us.

"It's probably nothing. In a few weeks,
They reckon everyone will have forgotten about it."

– *Day 340*

Americanised Cousins

I sometimes like to think about the literal translations of Chinese names for countries. You see, for most names, the Chinese language assigns characters that represent the closest sound to the original syllables. Here are some of my favourite literal translations:

*Finland—**Fēnlán*** *"Fragrance Orchid"*
*Portugal—**Pútáoyá*** *"Grape Tooth"*
*Tanzania—**Tǎnsāngníyà*** *"Flat mulberry tree, Asia"*

The word for America is **Měiguó**, which translates to "beautiful country."

Let's talk about the beautiful country.

In recent years, across Europe, I've noticed it becoming increasingly common to criticise America. While I completely accept the vast majority of the circulating criticisms, I believe I have developed a relationship with America that is a little more balanced, nuanced, and frankly, complicated. I hate it, sure. Above all, I hate its contradictions and hypocrisies. But I don't *only* hate it, because I love it too, insofar as I love its scenery, its spirit, its soul, and its creative projects, whether cinematic or musical. But I'm afraid it will take me another book to give this the full explication it deserves.

In China, the feelings towards America are *even more* complicated than my own. Especially among younger, urban, educated Chinese people, there's often admiration for things like American pop culture, innovation, tech, and higher education—many aspire to study in the States. People aren't afraid to admit that "**Měiguó de dàxué hěn hǎo**" (*American universities are very good*).

At the same time, there's a deep well of distrust and criticism, shaped by state media, which often frames the US as the arrogant interventionist unaware of its own interior decline. It is shaped by geopolitical tensions caused by all manner of developments—think Taiwan, trade wars, and military presence across the Pacific. It's also shaped by perceived hypocrisy over foreign policy, racial issues, and gun violence. Older generations, especially, might view America as a cautionary tale of chaos and decline.

For now, I'm not here to discuss the validity or oversight of any of these claims. This book is about China and *the world according to China.*

Some Chinese people admire the *idea* of America (freedom, prosperity, opportunity), but do not necessarily want to live there, and do not necessarily believe it works well in practice. They might say: "**Měiguó yǒu qián, dàn yě hěn luàn**" (*America is rich, but also chaotic*). It can generally be said that urban populations tend to be more open towards the US, while rural areas tend to be more suspicious, shaped mostly by domestic media narratives.

One thing that I found helpful was being told, "We distinguish between *the American government* and *American people.*" (It was here I felt the urge to hold up a mirror, having previously thought a very similar thing about China.) There's a strong tradition of Chinese hospitality toward foreign guests, including Americans, regardless of politics. So someone might grumble about the US as a country but speak fondly of Americans they've met while travelling.

While we're on the subject of China's views, you ought to know that, in my experience, Chinese people are generally warmer towards British people than Americans. But there's a difference. To Chinese people, America is a grizzly bear, to be admired and photographed only while keeping a wary distance. Britain is like a Labrador. Cute, adorable, even fashionable. Fun fact—the Union Jack was the second most common flag I saw while in China, after their own. I saw it on purses, prams, and cocktail umbrellas. People like to keep up to date with the royal family. They like to talk about the Oxbridge rivalry, and Downton Abbey, and how we drink our tea with milk and sugar, but it's all very stereotypical. Most of the Chinese people I met saw the nice parts of the UK, not the crime, not the poverty, not the relentless crises and scandals. But it didn't bother me much. People would normally mistake me for an American anyhow.

The reason China can focus on the niceties of Britain is that, in their eyes, since the handover of Hong Kong in 1997, we have not represented any real threat to them (apart from, perhaps, those moments when we have been a feather to America's arrow). In our time, despite everything, the United States of America is still the greatest rival—and therefore potential threat—to the People's Republic of China, both economically and militarily.

Still, it is fair to say a lot of young Chinese people admire America in some form. They have favourite rap stars. Favourite NFL teams. Favourite basketball players. NBA jerseys are a common sight in cities like Chongqing. The children I knew listened to Eminem and Taylor Swift—normally, without understanding the lyrics. They watched Marvel films in the cinema. One of my favourite things about living in China was being told I look just like sexy movie stars that I look nothing like... Robert Pattison, Zac Efron, Johnny Depp. They like to throw big names around like that.

Speaking of names. All Chinese kids get an English name to go with their Chinese one, and there are many different means of acquiring this name: (1) By sound or similarity—for example, a girl named *Mei* might choose May. (2) Lots of pupils are simply assigned names by their English teachers. "You are Kevin. You are Susan. You, Alan. Next, Dave. Next, Jimbob..." (3) Because it sounds cool—Cherry, Coco, Kitty, Tiger, Stone. Yes, these are all real names I came across. (4) The names of favourite celebrities, from Ariana to Elvis, from Leonardo to Jennifer. (5) Online name generators.

A name that kept coming up surprisingly often was Vivian. Why Vivian? Possibly because it hints at a Western prestige. You see, Chinese has no sound for 'V,' and so to a Chinese girl, Vivian sounds exotic, sleek, and cultured. Valerie, Vanessa, Vera, and Vicky were also common picks, but none greater than the mighty Vivian.

One of the people I met during my time in China was the cool, older cousin of my friends. English name "Seven." Yes, he was unironically called Seven, which also happened to be his lucky number. "God made the world in seven days" was his catch-phrase. (For the record, he was an atheist.)

Seven was in his late twenties. He always wore cargo trousers, big trainers with chunky soles, and oversized spell-out jumpers with various American place names: Atlanta, Tallahassee, Lafayette. His hair was bleached at the front, spiked, and gelled. He had this permanent, practiced, pearly smile, like he was constantly posing for a prom photo. He didn't speak much English, but whenever he did, he insisted on inserting American slang. "Yo man, what's up."

To his family and friends, he was the cool Americanised cousin. The cultured one who was always travelling. Who brought back strange candy. Who drove a souped-up car. Who could afford a new phone every year. He had the best hair. The best clothes. The best luck. Always talking about how they do things on the other side of the ocean.

But Seven seemed to believe in the idea of America more than America itself. And this is where the story folds over. Because just as many Westerners arrive in China and think they are finally entering the land of Confucius, red lanterns, kung fu monks and wise pandas, many Chinese people who look westward imagine the streets of New York, the sunshine of LA, the sound of Drake in the clubs, and the promise of an apartment, a business, a car (as if they're handed out on arrival).

But China is not a kung fu movie. And America is not an episode of *Friends*.

The truth is, both countries contain multitudes, and neither one really exists in the distilled versions we see through TikTok, Hollywood, or WeChat. Both have mythology. Both have masks. Both have complicated truths that eclipse the lens that can be placed upon them.

Seven, bless him, lived deep within the lens. He lived for the lens. He was the kind of guy who chose the 'blue pill' every single time. He was a product of both worlds: Chinese by birth, American by affectation. And he wasn't alone. There were many Sevens in China. It seemed to me that every wealthy family had a cool, Americanised cousin.

This chapter has been perhaps the most tangential. But my point is this: Part of what defines a nation is how it sees *other* nations. In China, there are options. You can be the sceptical grandma, the patriotic uncle, or the cool, westernised cousin. But few people allow for the possibility of nuance. And I would say the same of the West and how we view the rest of the world.

"When you love someone,
You love everything about them.
You love their talents and their quirks.
You acknowledge not only the promise of their future,
But the failures of their past.
And if you truly love someone,
You accept that they are complicated and flawed.
You don't solely simplify them into what you want them to be.
Neither do you solely believe the things people tell you about them.
You try your best to be with them, explore with them, and listen.
You help them achieve their potential
To do good in the world.
The same can perhaps be said of a nation."

– Day 328

Laojundong Temple

I visited many ancient and modern places of worship across the country. One of my favourites was back in Chongqing, overlooking the city from the great heights of Nan'an. Laojundong Taoist Temple.

It started with a bad hangover and a craving for elevation, both in spirit and altitude.

There's something about climbing a mountain that makes you feel like you're solving a problem—not with your mind, and not with your hands, but with your legs. I'd been in Chongqing for months, a city that already stacked buildings like Tetris blocks and cooked its food with more spice combinations than I had emotions to deal with them. But on this particular Sunday, I needed somewhere quiet. Somewhere ancient. Somewhere high enough above the traffic to feel like the horns and construction drills couldn't reach me.

Laojundong. Old Lord Cave. A Taoist temple dug into a mountain on the southeastern bend of the city. I'd passed the sign on a bus once and assumed it was one of those tourist traps with fake monks, actors, and overpriced incense. But a friend reckoned it was the 'real deal,' so I gave it a shot.

The walk from the bus stop was longer than I expected. First up a concrete road, then through a gate, then five hundred stone steps to the main hall. At first, I wasn't convinced. I could still hear the city. But the further I climbed, the quieter everything got. I could hear birds instead of scooters. Wind instead of loudspeaker ads. It was the first time in weeks the city had been silenced. This time by height rather than radius.

The temple, when I finally reached it, wasn't built so much as absorbed into the rock. Halls and stairways folded into the mountain's body like they had grown there. The walls were red with age and layered with incense ash, as though the whole thing had been exhaling for a thousand years. Statues of ancient Taoist immortals looked out with patient eyes. Gold Chinese characters everywhere—traditional Chinese, which I couldn't understand.

They say Laojundong has been around for over 1,300 years. That it started in the Sui or Tang dynasty, maybe even earlier if you believe the stories about the Three Kingdoms era. But buildings lie, and so do dynasties. What feels true is that the place is old in the same way mountains are old—weathered, scarred, but still standing.

The name comes from Laozi himself, the old master of Taoism who may or may not have been real, and who may or may not have ridden off on a green ox into the mountains to disappear. This, apparently, was one of the places into which he had vanished. But when Taoism rose and fell with the tides of Chinese empires, Laojundong remained—sometimes abandoned, sometimes rebuilt, sometimes renamed.

In 1480, it was reconstructed into a grand hall. By 1581, it had officially shifted from a Buddhist site to a Taoist one, called Taiji Palace, but still known by locals as Laojundong. Then, in 1739, under the Qing dynasty, it became part of the Quanzhen Dragon Gate sect—one of the largest branches of Taoism. Since then, it's held its position not just as a temple, but as *the* temple. They even call it *The First Taoist Monastery in Eastern Sichuan*, though that sounds like the kind of title you give yourself when no one else is paying attention.

But it deserves it. You can tell by the way even the loudest Chongqing native gets quiet when he walks through the main gate. Something ancient presses on your skin up there. Not in a spooky way—more like gravity. Like time has thickened around the stone.

The Sanqing Hall was rebuilt in 2009 but still smells like fire and dust. There are caves behind the buildings with names like Monkey Cave and Tushan Cave. Some of them have carvings older than any living person. One stone tablet shows nine dragons swirling in the clouds, another shows Laozi with his ox, smiling faintly like he knows something no one else does.

I sat on a bench near the top, beside an old woman who was, I think, muttering prayers under her breath. She didn't look at me once, which was rare in a country where most people saw my face and immediately assumed I was either a lost tourist or some sort of spy. For a few minutes, we shared the silence. I didn't know the prayers, but I tried to match her rhythm. Maybe that's Taoism: matching the rhythm of a place you don't understand, the rhythm of this inexplicable world.

On the way back down, I saw a boy of about eight throw a plastic bottle off the edge of the path. His mother tapped the back of his hand and made him climb into the bushes to fetch it. She said something like, "The gods will get angry."

I'm not sure if she was joking or just using it as a way to scare the child into picking up his litter, but either way, there was something about what she said that stuck with me. I guess I liked the idea of gods who got annoyed by litter. Who weren't floating above the world, but were actually in it—in the rocks, in the caves, in the soil. That, to me, felt more real than anything I'd ever read about Taoism. Maybe that's the point. You don't study it. You just walk into it. You climb some steps, breathe the incense, and let the mountain remind you that your hangover and your ego aren't as important as you think.

China is, officially, a secular country. You won't find much talk of gods or prophets in the classroom, or for that matter, in the office. Religion is permitted but carefully monitored. Temples operate, incense burns, rituals take place—but in my opinion, it's often unclear where spirituality ends and tourism begins.

Yet even in a nation of neon lights, skyscrapers, and electric mopeds, Taoism is still there. Not always in temples. Often in the corners of bookshelves, or tucked under beds, dust-adorned. I remember the little Taoist trinkets scattered across the house. A smooth jade pendant tied with red thread hung above the rice cooker. A small figurine of Laozi riding an ox, perched on the windowsill. A decorative knot with the Taiji symbol—Yin and Yang—dangling from the rear-view mirror of Shushu's car. He wasn't a religious man, per se, but he respected many of the teachings.

One evening, after dinner, Shushu came to my room with a book. He had a half-proud, half-embarrassed smile. "Daojia," he said. "Taoist teachings. You should know this. Maybe you can find peace, fortune, and happiness."

I sat up in bed, genuinely touched. I opened the book with anticipation, but I ran into a small problem—the entire thing was in German, not English. I didn't have the heart to tell him. I smiled and thanked him, and spent five very deliberate minutes flipping through the pages, nodding like someone reading the secrets of the universe. The book went on my shelf. It moved with me to three different apartments, and then beyond China.

I always told myself it didn't matter. That eventually I'd find the time to sit down and really learn about the wisdom of Taoism, and maybe Buddhism too. After all, I'd lived in a country where these philosophies thrive. I'd walked through smoky temples, bowed before ancient statues, eaten rice noodles beneath red lanterns glowing with mysticism. Surely, that gave me an obligation, if not an excuse, to learn more.

But years have passed, and I'm afraid to say, I've still not learned about the ancient wisdom. There's always something slightly more important to do, in my mind, whether it's a piece of work, an important email, spending time with friends, writing a book about China... well, maybe it's finally time.

In the days since China, back in England, I met a young Buddhist who just so happened to also be one of the coolest people I've ever met. He was my housemate for a year, along with a group of four of the most wonderful people I've ever *accidentally* moved in with.

Most of the time, he and I talked about music, or politics, or crappy early-noughties British comedies, but every so often, we would share something more profound. A conversation about something real. Our deeper anxieties, beliefs, and quandaries. He taught me about some of the principles of Buddhism, often by asking me questions that infuriated me because I could not satisfactorily answer them with my own logic. He even taught me how to meditate, or at least tried to.

Nothing about his life was easy. (For one thing, he dedicated it to helping other people by becoming a mental health nurse). But he was one of the happiest, most collected, most calming individuals I've ever had the privilege of knowing. He poured tea for me often, and in those moments, when the herbal scents hit me, it transported me back to China.

According to some statistics, Buddhism is the most practiced religion in China to this day (though it originated in India). But still, I felt like China was contacting me again. This time, not in the form of a text message, or a video call, but in the form of ancient teachings, told through a guitar-wielding housemate.

It's easy to fixate on robots, electronics, and plastic toys, but China is more than modernity. China is ancient, and its past is inseparable from its present and future.

We can disagree about how we got here or why, as millennia of conflicts have shown, but surely, we can agree that it's all pretty bloody amazing. Me, I'm grateful for a seat on this ride—however brief—through the universe. I'm grateful for nature. I'm grateful for family and friends. I'm grateful for tea. And I'm grateful for Kiran. Wherever you are, my friend, I wish you peace and prosperity, however you choose to define it.

"Just got back from the temple.
I'm back to the crazy world of flashing headlights,
Buzzing phones, and hundred-mile-an-hour train rides.
The temple is the only thing that's still, and I miss it already."

– Day 259

The Rap Capital

Chengdu wasn't even on my mental map before I visited. Sure, words like 'panda' and 'spice' had been thrown around, but I had no idea what waited beyond those clichés. What I found was unexpected: A city with a pulse and an attitude that felt like Chongqing's rebellious yet soulful big brother—the one who smokes clove cigarettes, designs his own clothes, disappears to Europe for tattoo lessons, then comes back with a swagger that defies explanation. This wasn't the China I thought I'd known.

Getting to Chengdu from Chongqing meant a sinuous, high-speed train ride that dipped through the mountain ranges that have been guarding secrets for centuries. The ride unspooled like a slow, unwinding thread, the landscape a quiet counterpoint to the frantic throb I was leaving behind in Chongqing. That city behind me was chaos incarnate, as you know—noisy, twisting, towering concrete puzzles stacked eight-dimensionally with millions squashed inside. Chengdu, by contrast, was a slow inhalation, a city holding its breath with a sly smile.

Alighting in Chengdu, I felt the vibe immediately. It hit me like a wok. You could tell the locals from the visitors by the way they dressed. People here owned their style. Jackets with cut and flow, drop-crotch pants, bucket hats. It was a city that ran on music and pure attitude. Walking into the streets felt like stepping into an underground music video, where every person, every storefront, every light fixture seemed perfectly choreographed. This was a city that wore its contradictions with pride. Modern skyscrapers cast long shadows over wooden shutters and tea houses where elders played mahjong under the faint scent of jasmine. The soundtrack? A clash of incongruously time-signatured bass lines weaving through the air.

The music itself was a revelation. Not the predictable pop or karaoke fodder, but something deeper, darker: Chinese hip hop that slapped basslines and rattled walls with Mandarin rhymes and Sichuanese swagger. I soon learned that hip hop in Chengdu was not only a form of art but a language of rebellion and belonging. It told stories of local struggles, of youth caught between tradition and modern life, and of a city refusing to be swallowed by the homogenised pop culture flooding the rest of the country. Each beat was a heartbeat, each rhyme a nuanced shout into the void that somehow echoed back with defiant joy.

One evening, wandering alone in what later turned out to be the Taikoo Li district, I practically fell into a basement bar humming with booming beats and neon lights. There was a kid on stage, mid-freestyle, Chinese flying off his tongue as if the words were projectiles. It wasn't polished. It wasn't MTV-ready. It was raw. Local dialect, slang-heavy, fierce. Words I didn't understand but felt between my ribs. The place was more than a bar; it was a sanctuary. Neon signs flickered with a signature mix of nostalgia and edge, and the sticky-sweet scent of incense mingled with the faint taste of burnt rubber from the old street outside. The energy was contagious, an embrace that pulled in everyone who walked through the door, whether they knew the words or not. Me, a **wài guó rén** in battered, tired trainers—I was part of something surprisingly intimate, a subculture strung together by freestyle verse and raw rhythm.

Chengdu isn't just another hot pot city. It's the cradle of Chinese hip hop, the unlikely birthplace of a movement that's reshaping culture. Ask the young heads in China, and they'll tell you: It all started here, not Beijing or Shanghai. That soft rebellion, the mix of tradition and defiance, felt utterly Chengdu. Graffiti sprawled boldly on railway pillars—not apologetic, not hidden. Cartoon pandas with grills, bubble letters, and Chinese characters shouting louder than the spoken word. What I learned from locals is that Chengdu's hip hop is inseparable from its culture—a blend of ancient Sichuan pride and youthful energy pushing boundaries. It's a sound propelled by beatnik originality but rooted deeply in tradition, a weird harmony between respect for the past and hunger for a new identity. Every lyric, every initial scratched into the wall, was a step in reclaiming space that often felt invisible in mainstream China.

Walking the riverside later that night, I found walls tagged from end to end. Names in English, in Mandarin. Local, foreign, alien. A street gallery where community and courage met paint. In a country where self-expression often lives inside lines drawn by governments, this felt like a whisper of freedom—soft, defiant, unmistakable. This riverside alley was a living, breathing gallery of expression. Among this rich tapestry, the line between outsider and local blurred, showing how art can carve out belonging in the hardest places.

At the hostel, I met a local who, half drunk and sipping warm beer from a busted fridge, said something that stuck with me: "In Chengdu, you don't have to be the best—you just have to be."

Every country has a city like this. *You know who you are.* Where you are a member of the city before you are a member of the country. Liverpool, Barcelona, Hamburg, Rio, Venice, Mumbai...

These are all stand-alone cities, distinct from the country that surrounds them. In China, for me, that city was Chengdu.

"Somewhere between Chongqing and Chengdu,
Somewhere deep in the mountains,
I must have fallen through a wormhole
Into another reality."

– Day 216

42C and 90% Humidity

Chongqing doesn't just have weather. It has a climate that imposes itself upon you like a tyrant. The first thing it takes from you is your dignity. Sweat is your new shadow. Shirts become towels. Showers become redundant the moment you step outside.

At the peak of August, your hair drooped instantly—and your sunglasses fogged over. This was a very specific kind of heat. It wasn't dry and airy like a desert. It was heavy. You were being swallowed, digested, and decomposed.

Locals had adapted in subtle but absolute ways: Their light mesh vests, the ever-present portable fans, the way they carried themselves in efficient, minimalist movements. The parks would fill up at 5 a.m. with tai chi groups moving in soft silence, hoping to catch the cool sliver of time before the air turned against them.

I once asked a friend what their favourite season was. "Winter," he said, without hesitation. "Because I can think clearly."

That's what this type of weather does. It dulls your brain. It short-circuits ambition. You don't want to work, write, argue, or dream. You want shade. Thus, daily life in Chongqing bends around the heat. People nap more. Lunch breaks stretch. Conversations slow. It's almost meditative. You are forced to acknowledge the limits of your body.

But step outside the city and the climate turns unrecognisable. China isn't just big. It's not just diverse. It's geographical theatre. A country of 1.4 billion people spread across 23 provinces (not counting autonomous regions and municipalities), each with a personality shaped by its landscape and weather.

In the Far North, you get the bone-dry winters of Heilongjiang and Inner Mongolia. There, the cold doesn't just nip, it gnaws. Harbin hosts an international ice festival where entire palaces are carved from frozen blocks. People wear fur-lined everything. Numbness is normal. The ground stays frozen until April.

Beijing, slightly further south, still freezes in winter, but with less severity. Summers, on the other hand, are dry and hot, and very, very, smoggy. Dust storms sometimes sweep in from the Gobi Desert, turning skies yellow and coating entire streets in sand.

Now, on the west side of the country, you have Xinjiang. A region of deserts, mountains, and political tension. Daytime highs in summer can hit 45°C in places like Turpan, and the toneless local dialect has even adapted to cope with this, flattening the tongue.

Down in Guangdong, in cities like Guangzhou and Shenzhen, the heat is more like Chongqing's—humid and punitive. But the South has its own rhythm. Cantonese food is lighter, steamier, and often served with cold tea that cools your insides. Locals know when to go slow.

Further west, bordering Vietnam, Laos, and Myanmar, we have the province of Yunnan, high in altitude and low in predictability. You can experience all four seasons in a single afternoon. One part of the day you're roasting under clear blue skies, the next you're running for cover from hail the size of quail eggs. Yet somehow, life there is gentler. The pace is slower, the air crisper, and the people more relaxed.

There's also Sichuan, neighbouring Chongqing, sharing much of its climate and spice tolerance. And on the East coast, in Shanghai and Jiangsu, you find a river delta heat, muggy and wet, with skies that seem eternally on the verge of tears.

What's striking is how these climates shape identity. The North has a reputation for being bold and brash. The South is seen as softer, more poetic. There is a perceived connection between land and lifestyle.

The majority of the population (about 90%) belongs to the Han ethnic group. But China is officially home to 55 other ethnic minorities, many of whom live in mountainous regions, beside long-disputed borders, where life is dictated not by national policy but by altitude and ancestry. In the Tibetan Plateau, villages have adapted to life at four thousand metres above sea level. Oxygen is thinner, nights are frigid, and the sun burns fast. People chew yak butter tea and carry prayer beads through the wind. In Guizhou, the Miao minority builds wooden stilt houses into steep green hills, holding onto rituals older than the country. In Zhuang communities, lush karst hills provide both beauty and barrier. And in the Far South, close to Vietnam, subtropical forests host Yao villages where songs are passed through generations orally.

Yet, despite all these differences—the languages, temperatures, cuisines, and landscapes—the whole country runs on a single time zone: Beijing Time. That means when the sun rises at 4:30 a.m. in Shandong, it also 'rises' simultaneously in Xinjiang, though the locals are still in complete darkness until 9 a.m. The political symbolism is hard to ignore: One country, one time, one centre of gravity.

In practical terms, it leads to all kinds of absurdities. Breakfast in Urumqi happens in darkness. Children walk to school in darkness. Streetlights flicker at noon. Locals adjust unofficially. You'll hear people refer to 'local time,' which often means ignoring their phone clock entirely. The sun might set at 11 p.m. in some regions, making summer nights feel endless. In Chongqing, it means late-night dinners on open rooftops, where people linger for hours over grilled fish and warm beer, the sky above still a brilliant shade of blue. It's one of those things you don't notice until you do—the way everyone carries on as if it's normal, even though it clearly isn't. But maybe that's the story of modern China in miniature: a set of contradictions that work only because enough people agree to keep going.

When I left Chongqing, I was glad to be rid of the forty-degree heat and ninety percent humidity. But I do miss the quiet heroism of life under it. The way it reshapes everything—how you move, what you eat, who you speak to, and when. It makes life feel more elemental. More immediate.

"I'm sweating out of places I never knew I could sweat.
This really is a journey of self-discovery."

– Day 56

The Revolving Restaurant

At first, I didn't realise we were moving. All I knew was that the restaurant was pretty damn high. Maybe it was because I didn't know the Chinese word for *revolve*, or maybe it was because the motion was so subtle. We sat down, ordered, and began eating, but something felt... *off*. I could have sworn that just a few minutes ago, I was looking at a grey office tower. But somewhere, somehow, it had slid out of view, replaced by a sprawling park and a snaking river. Ten minutes later, the scene shifted again—skyscrapers, highways, and the distant glint of the Pearl River sparkling under the sun.

That's when I understood. The restaurant was revolving. This was the 'Twist,' the highest revolving restaurant in the world, perched on the 106th floor of the Guangzhou CTF Finance Centre. The restaurant's rotation took exactly ninety minutes to complete a full three-sixty turn, allowing diners to enjoy an uninterrupted, panoramic feast for both eyes and palate without ever having to leave their seats.

China loves its revolving restaurants. You'll find dozens of them scattered across 'tier-one' cities and increasingly in smaller ones too. They're almost a signature architectural flourish—

symbols of status, progress, and the dazzling new China. While the Twist is the highest revolving restaurant in the world, cities like Chongqing, Shanghai, and Beijing all have their own versions. Many countries have them now, but to me, there is something particularly Chinese about this idea: A restaurant that doesn't stay put, a dining experience that mirrors a nation racing forward, never resting.

It's easy to assume that revolving restaurants are just about novelty—a gimmick to lure tourists or impress corporate clients, distracting them from dodgy transactions and Ponzi schemes. But the Twist felt like something more than that. The slow, effortless spin seemed like a metaphor for China itself. A country constantly in motion yet grounded; forever changing yet stubbornly the same at its core.

Dining in the Twist is an act of suspended disbelief. The sensation is surreal. From up there, the city below morphs and reinvents itself with every bite you take. Buildings, roads, and rivers slide gently past like scenes in a dream. The slow revolution disrupts your sense of stability, anchoring you in an unusual present where motion and stillness coexist.

The psychology of eating in a revolving restaurant is fascinating. On the one hand, you are a spectator—an observer of a world unfolding in a perfect circle, curated and controlled. On the other hand, you are part of the spectacle. You're not just watching the city; you're moving with it. The environment prompts reflection—a meditation on impermanence, and progress, and the broader experience of modern China. The country is an intricate balancing act of ancient tradition entwined with cutting-edge innovation, collectivism intertwined with fierce individual ambition, communism interwoven with capitalism, rapid urbanisation alongside pockets of rural stillness and nature. The revolving restaurant, high above the ground, spinning slowly but deliberately, captures that tension perfectly.

Eating in the Twist wasn't cheap. The food was not spectacular—it was, as is often the case with such places, the view and the experience you were paying for. The subtle movements, the evolving vista, the golden light that shifted with the angle of the sun—all those were a part of the meal *to distract you from the meal.* And in all fairness, they made it worth it. I've dined at many rooftop restaurants, but few have made the world itself feel like part of the cuisine.

The revolving restaurant is also a statement about China's aspirations and contradictions. It is flashy, ambitious, and undeniably showy, with an extravagant exterior and a drab interior. *"Isn't this all a bit OTT?"* you ask yourself after the entrée. A little too much? Yes. And yet, that excess is somehow inspiring. It reminds you that this is a country willing to dream big, to build tall, to spin the world beneath its feet.

In Western contexts, revolving restaurants are often seen as novelties—a fun gimmick for tourists or a once-in-a-lifetime experience. In China, however, they carry additional layers of meaning. They're status symbols, yes, but they're also collective experiences. The slow turn means the 'best seat' is never static. Everyone gets a chance to be in the spotlight. This egalitarian aspect ties back into the broader societal themes in China—the emphasis on community and shared progress, even in spaces of individual luxury.

The restaurant's design is democratic in a roundabout way. Unlike traditional fine dining spots where the best tables are fought over like gang turf and reserved for the privileged, here every seat eventually has the best view. (Though I'd argue anyone who can afford to dine there has some level of privilege.) Nevertheless, the revolving floor means there is no 'bad' table, no hierarchy of vantage points. The city is shared in full, rotating slowly for everyone. There's a certain poetic justice in that—a reflection, perhaps, of a society still wrestling with the balance between individual privilege and collective equality.

As we ate, I noticed a pair of newlyweds posing for photos near the windows. The bride wore a traditional red **qípáo** that shimmered in the soft light. The groom looked dapper but distracted, scrolling on his phone. They seemed to float in a moment suspended between tradition and modernity, much like the restaurant itself.

The more I thought about it, the more the Twist became a kind of symbol—for love, for life, for China. That slow, steady revolution felt like the passing of time itself, carrying us forward even as we stayed rooted in place. It was a reminder that nothing stands still, that change is inevitable and continuous, even when invisible. (Incidentally, my only note is that it should have revolved once an hour, like a clock hand, not once every ninety minutes. That just seemed ludicrous.)

This tension between collectivism and status, between egalitarianism and exclusivity, seems emblematic of China today. On one hand, you have an emphasis on shared progress and unity. On the other, a rapidly growing middle and upper class eager to distinguish themselves through experiences like dining in a skyscraper that turns. The restaurant's very existence is a statement of pride. It says, "Look how far we've come. Look at what we can build. This city, this country, can afford *things it doesn't need.*"

But there was a flip side. I couldn't help but feel a pang of melancholy for those who would never see the view from the Twist. For the millions living in Guangzhou's sprawling outskirts, in cramped apartments or rural villages, the restaurant wasn't a spectacle, or a symbol—it was just something they'd likely never experience.

The gulf between the dazzling heights of modernity and the often-difficult realities of daily life is vast. And yet, that gap exists everywhere, not just in China.

China is a country of paradoxical wisdom. I remember a conversation with my host family where we talked about **shíjiān jiùshì jīnqián** (*time is money*). It's a phrase that underpins much of modern China's drive. Yet it coexists with ancient sayings like **màn gōng chū xì huó** (*slow work yields fine craftsmanship*). That duality—speed and patience—is embodied perfectly in the Twist. It rotates slowly, deliberately, allowing you to take in the whole panorama, to savour the moment even as the city races below.

"Note to self: You don't need
To hire world-class chefs
If you have a world-class view."

– Day 310

The Foreigner Shop

Of course, it wasn't really called that. There was no official sign outside that said *Foreigner Shop*. No banner with a waving Union Jack or Statue of Liberty. The shop had a regular name—something generic like *Global Imports* or *International Delights*—but among expats, it was just the Foreigner Shop. As in: "I miss cheese. Let's go to the Foreigner Shop." Or: "I need peanut butter, the real kind, not the weird oily stuff. Foreigner Shop time."

I'm proud to say I only visited the place once. It was a particularly homesick Saturday afternoon. You don't always know when they're coming. Sometimes it's a smell, a whiff of fried onions or cold rain on concrete, and sometimes it's nothing. Just a full-body ache for something you can't name. That day, my Chinese family noticed I was quiet and a bit dejected, and instead of the usual attempts at distraction (hiking, hot pot, and karaoke), they bundled me into the car and said, with great solemnity, "We are taking you to the Foreigner Shop."

They didn't call it that, I don't think. But that's what it was.

The first thing I noticed inside was the air. It smelled like cardboard and nostalgia. There was a faint scent of cumin and paprika, of plastic wrap and freezer burn. The layout was chaotic, but the contents were nothing short of miraculous. A can of

Heinz baked beans. A dusty box of Yorkshire Tea. Pesto in a jar. Digestive biscuits. A small wedge of cheddar sealed in ten layers of plastic and priced like gold.

And Marmite.

God help me, Marmite.

The shelves were lined with foods that would be entirely mundane in their country of origin but had gained near-holy status through exoticism. A bottle of Ribena could fetch a small fortune. A box of Cheerios was considered a luxury item. And don't get me started on the imported chocolate. It was all there: Cadbury, Reese's, Lindt, even a Freddo.

My Chinese family wandered the aisles like anthropologists visiting a new world. They peered cautiously at jars of pickled onions and boxes of stuffing mix as if they might become the birth site of an alien invasion. My Chinese mum picked up a can of mushy peas, turned it over in her hands, and said, "Is this...a food?"

I nodded solemnly. "Yes. We eat it with fish and chips."

She looked utterly frightened.

It was the first time I saw Western food through someone else's eyes. Not Instagram food, not TikTok food. Not pizza or burgers or perfectly curated brunch plates. Real Western food. The kind you grow up with. The kind that lives in kitchen cupboards and gets lost in freezers for years. The kind that gets microwaved, mashed, and tinned. In their eyes, it was beige, and bland, and suspicious, and devastatingly unhealthy. To be fair, that wasn't completely false.

I decided to make them dinner.

Not a fancy one. I wasn't going to try and impress them—nor could I. Back then, I had still not learned how to cook properly. I wanted them to understand the normal stuff. The boring, comforting stuff. I wanted to show them the food that made me feel more like *me*. So I bought spaghetti, passata, basil, a bunch of vegetables, garlic bread (imported, stale, overpriced), and a block of parmesan so small it should've been illegal. Back home, I set to work boiling pasta and grating cheese, like it was a sacrament.

When I served the food, they were polite. Too polite. They smiled and said "thank you" in English and poked at it like it might scurry off the plate. I watched them take their first bites with the same nervous curiosity they'd shown the canned peas.

And you know what?

They didn't like it.

They didn't hate it, but they didn't like it either. They just didn't really *get it*. The brother added chilli oil. The dad drank hot water with it. The mum dissected it with chopsticks. It just wasn't the *same* in China.

But I didn't do it for them. I did it for me because I was missing home. Food is culture, yes. But more than that, it's *memory*. It's history, and habit, and identity, cooked at two hundred degrees Celsius. You can travel halfway across the world and learn a new language and fall in love with hot pot, and doufu gan, and red bean buns, but some part of you still wants fish fingers, baked beans, and a cup of milky tea. And that's not failure. That's just being human.

The Foreigner Shop reminded me of that. It wasn't just a shop. It was a little embassy of relief and longing. A place where you could buy overpriced sweets from your other life. A sanctuary for those moments when you're tired of translating, tired of adapting, tired of being the ambassador of your own existence. It was a place where I didn't have to explain myself.

But also, it wasn't mine anymore.

Not really.

That's the strange thing about living abroad. You change. You absorb things. You become fluent not just in a language, but in a way of being. And then, when you go back to the foods of your past, they feel off. Not bad, necessarily, just different. The spaghetti I made tasted like home, but also like a memory of home. My Chinese family didn't love it because it wasn't *their* comfort food. And in that moment, I realised it wasn't quite mine either.

We finished dinner. They washed the dishes. My Chinese mum said it was "interesting," which is the most generous word anyone has ever used for overcooked pasta. My Chinese brother made us all tea—green, not black—and we sat around the table together, full but not entirely satisfied.

That night, I thought about culture shock. Not the kind you get when you arrive, but the kind that hits when you realise you've changed. When you realise that you've started to miss things you didn't even know you liked, and when you go back to them, they feel hollow.

In the end, the Foreigner Shop didn't cure my homesickness, but it helped me to make peace with it. Homesickness, I've learned, isn't just about wanting to go back. It's about trying to carry all your past lives with you. Trying to stitch together the pieces of where you've been and who you've become. It's messy, and complicated, and sometimes comes in the form of an overpriced jar of Nutella.

"When you get back home,
It's pretty much how you left it.
But you have completely changed,
Such that your home no longer
Recognises you."

– Day 310

The Communal Cat

There's something about a cat that makes me feel calm. China can be disorienting at first—fast, unfamiliar, endless—but the presence of a friendly animal, one that purrs under your hand and blinks at you slowly, is a small anchor. I'd find myself crouching beside flowerbeds or stooping to give them a scratch behind the ears. One climbed into my lap while I was eating breakfast on a plastic stool. Another followed me home once, only to shy away at the last second and disappear down an alleyway.

There's something beautifully unbothered about cats. They don't care about your accent or visa status. They don't care much about you in general, to be honest. They're narcissists. But they're cute narcissists, and more importantly, they lower blood pressure and make you feel at home.

In China, there is a phenomenon I like to call the Communal Cat. Owned by no one. Fed by everyone. You see them in gardens, noodle shops, and perched on rooftops.

There was this one cat I remember vividly. It lived outside the back gate of my university, curled up like a discarded scarf beneath a bicycle rack. Every day on my way to class, I'd spot it nestled in the same spot, calmly watching the world. The students would throw it scraps from their breakfasts—youtiao, fried egg, pieces of sausage tucked in steamed buns, and sometimes someone would leave out a little saucer of milk.

She was a Calico. Scruffy but proud. Her tail flicked with purpose. I never saw her beg. She purred, like happy cats are meant to. She had, somehow, inserted herself into the rhythm of campus life, as if she had tenure. She had no name. She was just **Māo**, the Chinese word for cat.

There was another, a tomcat, that lived in a noodle shop near my flat. He lived in a cardboard box on a high shelf. You would often see his tail hanging down like a light switch. This one was less sociable—thin and wiry with a mottled silver coat turned grey, always winding between plastic stools and poking its head through the open doorway, cautiously. The shop owner never scolded it. Sometimes I'd see the man squat down and feed it tiny slivers of pork with chopsticks.

But not all cats were so lucky.

Sometimes I saw them darting across the road, thin and feral, with patches of fur missing and eyes clouded with infection. Once, while walking near the outskirts of the city, I passed a construction site and saw a pile of kittens curled beneath some corrugated metal. They were trembling. No food, no mother in sight.

Another time, I spotted a cat that had clearly been hit by a car. Its body was still in the road, while people walked around it with their eyes forward, unmoved. I stood there for a while, unsure of what to do. I couldn't even get to it because of the relentless flow of traffic.

Cats have it bad. Dogs have it worse.

In Chongqing, I once saw a dog tethered to a motorbike while its owner went inside to eat. It wasn't tied *beside* the bike—it was tied *to* the back of it, by the neck, leash stretched tight, panting in the midday sun. I stood nearby for ten minutes, trying to cool the dog with the shade of my body, but when the owner returned, he just laughed and waved me off like I was a child. "It's fine," he said. "Strong dog. Strong animal."

There is a stray animal problem in China that's easy to overlook but impossible to ignore once you notice it. Especially in the cities. Especially with dogs. You see them in alleyways, rooting around bins, trotting across intersections like ghosts. Most are thin. Many are sick. Some are aggressive—not because they're 'bad,' but because no one has ever been kind to them.

A lot of them were once pets. People buy dogs on a whim, especially small designer breeds—Pomeranians, Poodles, Shiba Inus. But when they grow too big, or bark too much, or get sick, they're discarded. Left on the street. Sometimes they're tied to trees outside train stations. Sometimes they're just driven to a different neighbourhood and abandoned like furniture. It's not everyone. Some humans are kinder. The life of an animal, anywhere in the world, is unfortunately highly contingent on the humans in the world.

In any case, animal welfare is still, broadly speaking, not a mainstream concern in China. There are no comprehensive national laws against animal cruelty. Some cities have bylaws, some provinces are trialling regulations, but it's patchy at best. Abuse is rarely punished, neglect is common, and abandonment is normal.

Some people simply don't see animals as beings with feelings. That's not to say they're unkind—it's cultural, systemic, and generational. In rural areas, animals have always been functional: Dogs guard property, cats catch rats, and mules cart cargo. Emotion is inefficient. In that world, a dog isn't your 'baby' or your 'best friend.' It's an asset, and if it stops being an asset, you get rid of it.

In wealthier urban centres, that's changing. I met plenty of Chinese people who adored their pets—who dressed them in tiny outfits, who brought them to cafés, who celebrated birthdays. But alongside this growing pet culture, there's also a rising tide of abandonment. The pet industry is booming. The rescue infrastructure is not. And what a lot of wealthy pet owners struggle to realise is that, generally speaking, a poodle doesn't *enjoy* being dressed up in silly clothing.

There are grassroots shelters, of course—some run by kind retirees, others by scrappy NGOs. But they're often underfunded and overwhelmed. I visited one in the suburbs once. A converted warehouse, full of cages and an endless choir of barking. The woman who ran it told me she had over two hundred dogs and thirty cats. She was feeding them all with her pension. She cried when I offered her a bag of food.

Then there's the flip side of all this: The intentional cruelty. Some people hurt animals for sport. It's extremely rare, but it happens. Videos have circulated of dogs being beaten, poisoned, and even skinned alive. In some markets, animals are kept in appalling conditions—crammed in cages and covered in sores. The infamous Yulin Dog Meat Festival still happens every year, despite mounting protests. And while many Chinese citizens oppose it, it's not banned.

Let's be clear: Not everyone in China treats animals so poorly. Many don't. Many love them. But as a system, as a society, animal life is undervalued—and this chapter is hard to write because I saw it. I walked past it. I couldn't unsee it. It's one of the rare things that made me feel genuinely proud of where I was from. I come from a country where animal welfare isn't just talked about but is actually implemented. In Britain, for *most* people, animals are more than objects. They're souls. More so, in fact, than most other places in the world that I have visited so far. If we are going to be proud of anything in the UK, then perhaps it can be of this simple fact.

The way a society treats its animals—regardless of how it uses them—tells you an awful lot about that society.

There's a kind of numbness that sets in when you're surrounded by suffering. Not because you're cruel, but because you have no power. What do you do when you see a stray bleeding in the road? Or a dog tied up so tightly it can't sit down? You want to help, but to what extent do you endanger yourself and enrage locals in a country that is not yours? So you walk past. And you hate that you do. But you do.

But at least there's this: China is a country in motion. It is changing faster than almost any other place in the world. In just a few decades, it has shifted from rural poverty to futuristic urbanisation, from coal smoke to solar panels. Advocacy is growing. Public health campaigns are booming. Education is on the rise.

And I hope—deeply, sincerely—that animal welfare becomes part of that future, even if it's in a small way. I hope that even more of the next generation grows up understanding that a cat is not a pest, a dog is not a tool, and life—regardless of species—deserves dignity. Ironically, this is something I believe that many ancient cultures, including the ones that existed in China, understood very well. Clearly, the roots of this particular plant of wisdom were buried too deeply in the soil.

Some of the signs are promising. I met Chinese teenagers who ran campus cat rescue accounts, who raised money for neutering strays, who tried to find homes for abandoned kittens. I saw dog cafés. Pet hospitals. Public outcry when news of cruelty spread online.

It's there. The empathy. The momentum. But it needs more than kind individuals. It needs systems. Laws. Education. It needs a shift in thinking, not just among young people in Beijing, but across villages and cities alike. Because there are too many suffering animals. Too many stories that never make it to paper.

I hear people say things like, "There are too many suffering people to worry about suffering animals," and I sympathise with that logic, but being kind to a dog doesn't mean you have to start being an arsehole to *people*. While humans are the solution to most of our problems, we are also the *cause* of most of our problems, and an animal has no idea about any of that. It's not their fault. They're just uncomprehending lives. Lives that bring colour to our world. I believe we are judged (somewhere, somehow) by how we treat those who are less intelligent than we are.

I still think about that little grey feline outside the noodle shop. I remember how it climbed onto my lap one day, uninvited, purring like a little motor, like a hand-held electric fan. I remember how the shop owner smiled when he saw us. He didn't say anything. He just nodded and kept chopping onions.

I stayed there for a long time, slurping my noodles slowly, with the cat curled up on my lap. Maybe the future starts in moments like that.

"Look, it's quite simple:
I was having a bad day.
Cat sat on my lap.
Now I'm having a good one."

– *Day 95*

PEK Terminal 3
(Final Thoughts)

China is not a country that offers itself up all at once. It doesn't greet you at the arrivals gate with a well-practiced smile and a welcome drink. As I stood at the gates of Beijing International Airport (PEK Terminal 3), I realised it didn't wave you goodbye either. It was far too busy. China was uninterested in being legible, or consistent, or comfortable. It didn't care if you understood it. In fact, I often got the feeling it rather hoped you wouldn't.

This is not to say that China is unfriendly. In fact, I found generosity there in impossible places: In clothing stalls run by old women who refused my money. In taxi drivers who went miles out of their way because they were worried I'd get lost. In colleagues who invited me into their homes like I was a cousin they hadn't seen in years. But for every warm act of kindness, there was also bureaucracy that made no sense, air that clung to my throat like tar, or sudden, stony silence when I asked too much about the wrong topic.

After a year, I couldn't say I understood China any more than I understood computational mathematics. After half a decade of reflection, I *still* can't. I can only say that I experienced it, and that I lived inside its contradictions for a little while. I watched its cranes swing the steel bones of tomorrow's buildings through the air. I heard old men slap cards down onto cracked plastic tables while chain-smoking cigarettes beneath red banners.

It is difficult to write a conclusion about a place that never ends, and I therefore almost didn't bother writing this chapter. But things always have some kind of conclusion, don't they?

The China I knew was noisy. It was a cloud of steam, a kaleidoscope of dazzling lights, and a fan that never quite reached you. It was three-wheeled taxis grinding their way up mountainsides. It was a place where I was almost never alone, even when I wanted to be.

I came to China with ideas: It was authoritarian, crowded, cheap, efficient, mysterious, powerful, dangerous; that it was to be interpreted, dissected, explained... All of that was wrong, and all of that was right. China taught me that there are many truths in this world, not a single truth. It's a scary thought, but it explains a lot.

The problem was the simple-minded premise that a place could ever be one thing, or that 1.4 billion people could be summed up by a string of adjectives. That a country with 5,000 years of written history could be understood in the span of a single visa.

On the Chinese flag, the four small stars stand for the social classes, the big one stands for the Communist Party. Together, it represents unity. Like all flags, it's a symbol that tells a story. But just like the stories we tell *ourselves* about the countries we live in, it's a simplification. The China I knew was far from unified. It was both fractured and stitched together, ancient and brand new, aching with the weight of its own scale.

It is a country constantly arriving, and it's always arriving late. But at the same time, it's a decade before its time. But perhaps that is too simple a metaphor. Too Western a lens. We like stories that move forward, progress that can be measured. China's story doesn't fit neatly into our arcs. It is circular, recursive, and patient. It doesn't explain itself. And sometimes, it doesn't even know itself. It's still looking down on itself, *discovering* itself from the sky rails, from the mountain tops, from the revolving restaurants, and from the bedrooms of fifty-ninth floors. In this way, I like to think I am a small part of this discovery.

There were days in China when I hated it. When I got scammed or censored. When the air made my eyes sting and my throat close. When I couldn't say what I wanted to say, either because I didn't have the vocabulary or because I wasn't allowed to say it. When I saw dogs with broken legs, dragging themselves across the road, or children coming home from school past 9 p.m., barely able to keep their eyes open.

And yet I stayed. Because there were also days when I loved it. When I watched couples dancing in the park. When I saw, heard, or even tasted something that changed my perspective. After all, 'perspective' and 'travel' are near synonyms. I stayed for all the times I laughed at a joke that made sense differently in two languages. For when I felt—just for a second—that I belonged.

If I learned anything from that year, it's that the job of living in another country isn't to translate it. It's to witness it. To sit with the confusion, the contradiction, and the constant sense that you are both too close and too far away.

China is not a monolith. It's not a puzzle box. It's not a dragon, or a wall, or a red tide. It's just sky, land, and the people in between.

When I first arrived in China, someone told me the country was like an onion. You peel back a layer and cry. And then you peel back another layer, and cry again. By the time you get to the core, you're kind of used to it. You see the beauty in it. You realise that it can create wonderful things… as the starting ingredient of many recipes… Is that right? I don't know, I've lost the metaphor now.

Either way, I don't think I ever reached the core of that 'onion.' This book isn't meant to explain China. As if it ever could. It is, however, meant to *remember* China. It is a whistle-stop tour of one particular experience of China. It is meant to give you some ideas—some inspiration, perhaps, to go and find your own experience of the country, or of Asia, or of anywhere.

It is not an exaggeration to say my life would be completely different had I not gone to China, not only because of the bible's worth of lessons I learned, and not only because of the friends I made, but because going to China led to a chain of events that brought me to this precise location in space and time. It gave me confidence, qualifications, and insights that I would never have otherwise had.

Because large sums of my income go towards travel (to the detriment of more 'important' things), I've been to quite a few places in my twenty-odd years. None of them can hold a candle to China's strange allure, vortex, liminality, anachronism, and *heft*.

Do you recommend China?

I get this a lot.

For a holiday? No. For beach-side relaxation? No. For enrichment, astonishment, and a world-tilting reality shift? Yes, absolutely. Go, now. I recommend two things, in fact: (1) Go to China, and (2) live with a Chinese family there.

Which reminds me, before I close the book on this chapter of my life, I need to acknowledge how lucky I am, not only to have been boarded by the Lee family, not only to have been welcomed into their home, but to be welcomed into their family. I miss them.

Beijing was once known by two other names: *Beiping* and *Peking*. The latter explains Beijing International Airport's 'PEK' airport code. I realised this as I waited for my flight at Terminal 3, on the last day of my stay.

At some point, and I don't remember exactly when, I wrote this in the notes app on my phone:

"Before I left for China,
I struggled to get my visa approved.
I struggled to make the trip logistically feasible.
But more importantly,
I started second-guessing my decision.
I was terrified, indifferent, lazy.
It was going to be a lot of effort, and for what?
I nearly never got on that plane at Heathrow.
Now I can see that I was right.
I would have saved myself
A lot of bother if I had stayed home...
And what a tragedy that would have been."

– Day 365

Acknowledgements

A huge thank you to the family who looked after me while I was in China, who treated me as one of their own despite my largely overt Westernness. They sustained me for a year. I don't just mean that in terms of food and accommodation, but in terms of informal education—many of the valuable lessons I learned abroad I can attribute directly to them. In particular, I would like to thank Shushu and Ayi.

Secondly, I would like to thank my own family (my English family), who, despite initial concerns—and frankly, shock—were ultimately supportive in my decision to leave the country as soon as I finished school and journey 5700 miles to a strange land where they would not be able to see me for a year. Many parents look at mine and conclude that their willingness to allow me to travel so far on my own and to put myself in potential danger is a clear sign that they are irresponsible. They conclude that they don't *care* about me. But the truth is, it's *because* they care about me that they allowed me to travel so far alone and to put myself in potential danger. I submit that anything worth doing is not entirely safe. There is always risk in development. There is risk in adventure, there is risk in discovery, and there is risk in love.

I would, reluctantly, like to thank Caistor Grammar School for giving me the type of education that dares to think beyond the world in which we live. Despite accumulating more detentions and more expulsions—and certainly causing more chaos—than anyone else in my year group, a *couple* of individuals continued to believe in me. For this, I'd like to thank former headmaster Roger Hale, who inspired me to use writing, music, and curiosity to overcome the darker things. I maintain that he is the greatest headmaster the school has ever seen, even in its four hundred years of history.

I should also, therefore, thank the school I mistakenly attended for sixth form (which shall remain nameless), where I hated, and was hated by (or at least unwelcomed by) the majority of its staff and students, such that it contributed to two of the worst years of my life. I was angry, alone, and acutely depressed, and while most of that can be blamed on other circumstances that originated outside of school, I would still like to thank the school for its contributions in this, for without it, I would not have had the drive to *get away,* far away to a distant land. (In a more neutral tone: I'm not actually blaming the school itself, but *my* individual experience of the school. It is true, however, that without this difficult period of my life, I would probably never have gone to China.)

In addition, I would like to thank (in the order in which we met), the following individuals for being a small but notable part of the motivation for this book, whether that is because they encouraged my writing or my adventures: Shirley Levy, Lucy Hand, James McBain, Callum Connor, Daisy Johsnon, Alistair Graham, Jaye Moore, Alexis Atmadjov, Mark Thomspon, Kelsey Lambert, Kiran Evetts, Thomas Karshan, and Emily Haworth.

About the Author

Sam Levy is a writer from Lincolnshire, UK. After studying Chinese at Chongqing Technology and Business University, he moved on to complete a course in English Literature at the University of East Anglia. He is currently in his final year of a Speech and Language Therapy master's degree at the University of Lincoln. His previous projects include the novel *Fresh Start 40,* but he has since branched out into the world of non-fiction, debuting with *Notes from the 59th Floor.*

Quick Note from the Author:

Hēi**! If you enjoyed this book, consider rating it on Amazon or Goodreads. As this is my first published work of non-fiction, it would mean a great deal to me. Thank you.* ***Xièxiè. *More books on the way...*

@sam.le.vy